Cotswolds Travel Guide 2025/2026

Explore England's Quintessential Countryside Walks, Villages, Food, and Itineraries for Every Season...With Maps And Photos

Jet Setterson

Copyright © 2025 by Jet Setterson

All rights reserved. No part of this publication may be copied, reproduced, stored in a retrieval system, or transmitted in any form or by any means—electronic, mechanical, photocopying, recording, or otherwise—without the prior written permission of the author, except in the case of brief quotations used in reviews or academic works.

This guide is intended to provide accurate, up-to-date information about destinations, travel logistics, and visitor experiences as of the time of publication. While every effort has been made to verify the content, changes can occur in travel conditions, pricing, contact details, laws, and local regulations. The author disclaims any liability for loss, damage, or inconvenience caused as a result of reliance on the material herein.

Use this book as a starting point for planning your journey, but confirm all critical details independently. Travel responsibly and stay informed about health, safety, and legal requirements relevant to your destination.

First Edition, 2025

Jet Setterson.

Table of Contents

Chapter 1: Introduction.. 5
  About This Guide..5
  Why Visit the Cotswolds?...5
  What's New in 2025/2026..7
  Quick Planning Overview...8
  Top 10 Experiences in the Cotswolds..9

Chapter 2: Essential Travel Information... 12
  When to Visit: Seasonal Guide... 12
  How to Get to the Cotswolds... 14
  Getting Around the Cotswolds... 19
  Where to Stay: Accommodation Guide.. 21
  Local Etiquette & Safety.. 28
  Language & Communication Tips.. 29

Chapter 3: Regions & Villages Of The Cotswolds.. 32
  Overview of Cotswolds Geography & Layout..32
  Northern Cotswolds Highlights..33
  Central Cotswold Highlights..39
  Southern Cotswolds Highlights: Cirencester — The Capital of the Cotswolds........47
  Eastern Cotswold..53
  Western Cotswold & Outskirts...58

Chapter 4 : Experiences & Themes... 63
  Walking & Hiking Trails..63
  Gardens, Manor Houses & Historic Sites.. 65
  Food & Drink in the Cotswolds.. 67
  Market Towns & Artisan Shops... 69
  Festivals & Seasonal Events (2025/2026 Calendar)................................71
  Literary, Arts & Film Locations.. 73
  Family-Friendly Activities.. 77
  Romantic Getaways & Luxury Retreats In The Cotswolds...................... 79
  Sustainable & Eco-friendly Travel In The Cotswolds.............................. 80

Chapter 5: Curated Itineraries.. 82
  3-Day Cotswolds Highlights Itinerary.. 82
  5-Day Slow Travel & Hidden Gems Itinerary... 83
  7-Day Classic Cotswolds Road Trip Itinerary...84
  10-Day In-Depth Cultural & Scenic Cotswolds Route.............................. 86
  Seasonal Itineraries in the Cotswolds:.. 87

Chapter 6 : Practical Tips & Resources.. 92
  Packing Guide for All Seasons... 92

- Accessibility Information..93
- Traveling with Pets in the Cotswolds...94
- Photography Tips & Best Viewpoints in the Cotswolds...95
- Emergency Contacts & Healthcare in the Cotswolds..96
- Local Tour Operators & Experiences in the Cotswolds...97
- Cotswolds Souvenirs & What to Bring Home..99

Appendices..103
- Glossary of Local Terms & Phrases in the Cotswolds...103
- Annual Events Calendar 2025–2026..105
- Public Transport Timetables: Key Routes in the Cotswolds...106
- Driving & Parking Guide for the Cotswolds..108

Map

Chapter 1: Introduction

About This Guide

This Cotswolds Travel Guide 2025/2026 is designed to provide travelers with an in-depth, expert-level exploration of one of England's most beloved regions. Whether you're a first-time visitor looking to capture the essence of the English countryside, or a returning traveler seeking out lesser-known corners and immersive experiences, this guide offers practical, up-to-date advice to help you plan a memorable and meaningful trip.

Unlike generic travel resources, this guide includes:

- Detailed profiles of more than 40 towns, villages, and hamlets—beyond just Bourton-on-the-Water and Stow-on-the-Wold.
- Hidden gems, including secluded walking trails, overlooked manor houses, and charming farm cafés locals frequent.
- Curated itineraries for different travel styles—romantic escapes, slow travel, foodie adventures, and family trips.
- Seasonal insights highlighting what to do and where to go at different times of the year, from lavender fields in summer to Christmas markets in December.
- Transportation tips tailored to both drivers and non-drivers—covering trains, buses, and walkable village routes.
- Up-to-date information for 2025 and 2026, including festival schedules, opening hours, costs, and sustainability options.

This guide is grounded in local knowledge and field research, reflecting the latest travel conditions, business updates, and cultural developments post-pandemic and post-Brexit.

Why Visit the Cotswolds?

The Cotswolds is a designated Area of Outstanding Natural Beauty (AONB), spanning nearly 800 square miles across five counties:

Gloucestershire, Oxfordshire, Warwickshire, Wiltshire, and Worcestershire. This enchanting region is characterized by rolling hills, honey-coloured limestone villages, historic market towns, and timeless English charm.

Here are just a few reasons to make the Cotswolds a centerpiece of your UK travel plans:

1. Quintessential English Scenery

The Cotswolds is what many envision when they think of the "English countryside." Think stone cottages with climbing roses, gently undulating meadows dotted with sheep, dry-stone walls, and winding country lanes. It's a place where the landscape feels like it's been lifted straight from a postcard—or a period drama.

2. Deep Historical Roots

From medieval wool churches and Roman roads to Jacobean manor houses and Neolithic burial sites like Belas Knap, the Cotswolds tells the story of rural England across the ages. Several towns—such as Cirencester and Tetbury—date back to Roman and Saxon times and are filled with architectural heritage.

3. Walkable Villages and Countryside Trails

The region is home to some of Britain's finest walking paths, including the 102-mile Cotswold Way National Trail, which stretches from Chipping Campden to Bath. Whether you're looking for a leisurely riverside stroll or a more rugged hilltop hike, the Cotswolds offers trails suitable for all levels and seasons.

4. Food, Drink & Artisan Culture

The Cotswolds is a food-lover's dream, offering everything from Michelin-starred dining (e.g., Le Manoir aux Quat'Saisons nearby in Great Milton) to rustic pubs serving locally brewed ale and seasonal fare. Farm shops, cheesemongers, bakeries, and weekly markets are integral to village life. It's also a region of thriving artisan workshops, galleries, and antiques.

5. Slow Travel & Rural Luxury

The pace of life in the Cotswolds is delightfully unhurried. This makes it ideal for travelers seeking relaxation, wellness, and reconnection with nature. You'll find luxury spa hotels, cozy fireplaces in historic inns, and wellness retreats in manor estates. At the same time, there are plenty of affordable self-catering cottages and eco-lodges for budget-conscious and sustainable travelers.

6. Year-Round Beauty

The Cotswolds is not just a summer destination. Spring brings lambs to pasture and gardens in bloom. Autumn sets the beech woodlands alight with gold and copper. In winter, the region transforms into a cozy wonderland, complete with roaring pub fires, Christmas markets, and frost-covered hills. Many travelers return in different seasons for fresh perspectives.

Whether you're visiting for a weekend escape from London or planning a weeklong countryside adventure, the Cotswolds offers something for everyone—history lovers, walkers, foodies, families, and solo travelers alike. This guide will help you explore its most iconic sites and uncover its best-kept secrets, creating a trip that goes beyond the ordinary.

What's New in 2025/2026

While the Cotswolds is steeped in timeless charm, the region is constantly evolving—introducing new events, attractions, accommodations, and infrastructure improvements. Here are the latest developments and trends to be aware of for your 2025–2026 visit:

1. New and Revamped Attractions

- **Cotswold Farm Park Expansion (Spring 2025)**

    Adam Henson's popular family-friendly farm has added an eco-education centre and rare breeds walking loop, enhancing both its sustainability credentials and interactive visitor experiences.

- **Cirencester Roman Amphitheatre Upgrades**

    English Heritage completed subtle conservation enhancements in 2024, including new interpretive signage, improved walking paths, and augmented reality features via mobile app integration.

- **Broadway Tower Bunker Experience 2.0**

    The revamped Cold War bunker beneath Broadway Tower reopened in late 2024 with updated interactive displays, a new guided audio tour, and timed ticketing for smoother visitor flow.

2. Transport & Accessibility Improvements

- **Electric Bus Pilot Scheme (Gloucestershire Cotswolds)**

    A new low-emission shuttle bus trial, connecting Bourton-on-the-Water, Stow-on-the-Wold, and Moreton-in-Marsh, began in summer 2024 and continues in 2025. Ideal for car-free travelers.

- **Cotswold Way Digital Trail Companion**

    Walkers can now use a dedicated free app with real-time trail mapping, historical facts, and emergency access points. Especially useful for solo walkers and international visitors.

- **More EV Charging Points**

    Over 30 new EV charging stations have been installed in car parks across Cirencester, Stroud, and Broadway—supporting the rising number of electric vehicle visitors.

3. Accommodation Highlights

- **Opening of Wildflower Barns, Near Kingham (2025)**

    A collection of off-grid, solar-powered luxury barns offering immersive countryside stays with foraging and wellness workshops.

- **Restoration of The Bear Inn, Bisley (Reopened 2024)**

    A 17th-century coaching inn brought back to life with sustainable materials, farm-to-table dining, and dog-friendly rooms.

4. Events & Cultural Additions

- **The Cotswold Arts Festival Launch (Summer 2025, Chipping Norton)**

    A new annual celebration of rural and contemporary art, artisan crafts, and open-studio trails, expanding local creative tourism.

- **Anniversary Celebrations: Westonbirt Arboretum at 200**

    The National Arboretum celebrates its bicentenary with a packed 2026 program of exhibitions, guided forest walks, and botanical showcases.

Quick Planning Overview

Here's a streamlined guide to help you start planning your Cotswolds adventure, tailored for both short visits and extended stays in 2025/2026.

Best Time to Visit

- **Spring (March–May):** Lambing season, wildflowers, fewer crowds. Ideal for gardens and countryside walks.

- **Summer (June–August):** Peak season with lavender fields, festivals, and the best weather. Book early.

- **Autumn (September–November):** Stunning foliage, apple harvests, and quieter villages. Great for foodies.

- **Winter (December–February):** Cosy pubs, Christmas markets (like Cirencester and Cheltenham), and fewer tourists.

How Many Days?

- **3 Days:** Perfect for a highlights trip (e.g., Bourton, Broadway, Stow-on-the-Wold).
- **5–7 Days:** Allows exploration of multiple villages, walking trails, manor houses, and markets.
- **10+ Days:** Ideal for deep travel, including wellness stays, walking holidays, and slower-paced exploration.

Getting There

- **By Train:** Direct trains to Moreton-in-Marsh, Kemble (for Cirencester), and Stroud from London Paddington (approx. 1.5–2 hours).
- **By Car:** Essential for full flexibility. Rent a car from London, Oxford, or Birmingham for easy access to villages.
- By Tour: Day tours from London or Bath available for those short on time, but less immersive.

Getting Around

- **Car Rental:** Recommended for flexibility; many roads are narrow and scenic.
- **Public Transport:** Bus routes exist but are limited in frequency—check timetables carefully.
- **Walking & Cycling:** Ideal in good weather; many villages are walkable, and trails like the Cotswold Way offer scenic routes.

Top Booking Tips

- Reserve accommodation early (especially for weekends, summer, and holidays).
- Check for seasonal opening times, especially for smaller attractions and gardens.
- Use local apps for walking trails, parking, and pub reservations many now require booking ahead, even in rural areas).

Top 10 Experiences in the Cotswolds

The Cotswolds is more than just postcard-perfect villages—it's a living cultural landscape with centuries of history, outstanding natural beauty, and experiences that offer something for every type of traveler. These are the ten essential experiences that define a truly unforgettable visit to the region:

---

1. Walk the Cotswold Way National Trail

Stretching 102 miles (164 km) from Chipping Campden to Bath, the Cotswold Way is a long-distance footpath that weaves through rolling hills, woodlands, and historic towns. Even if you don't walk the full trail, sections like the Broadway to Stanton loop or Painswick to Slad offer stunning day hikes. You'll pass Iron Age hill forts, ancient beech forests, and limestone escarpments with sweeping views.

- **Best for:** Hikers, photographers, nature lovers
- **Tip:** Download the Cotswold Way Companion App for maps, navigation, and historical points of interest.

---

2. Visit Bibury – The Quintessential English Village

Famed for Arlington Row, a line of 14th-century weavers' cottages that has become one of the most photographed scenes in England, Bibury sits on the banks of the River Coln. Though it can get crowded in peak season, an early morning or off-season visit allows you to enjoy its storybook charm in peace.

- **Best for:** First-timers, history buffs, architecture lovers

- **Tip:** Stop by Bibury Trout Farm, one of England's oldest working trout farms, and enjoy a riverside picnic.

---

3. Explore Historic Market Towns Like Cirencester and Tetbury

Cirencester, once the second-largest Roman city in Britain (Corinium), offers a rich blend of Roman ruins, medieval churches, and a lively weekly market. Nearby Tetbury is known for its royal connections (King Charles III's Highgrove estate is just outside the town) and its antiques quarter.

- **Best for:** History enthusiasts, shoppers, cultural travelers
- **Tip:** Don't miss the Corinium Museum in Cirencester, which holds one of Britain's finest Roman collections outside London.

---

4. Discover the Lavender Fields at Cotswold Lavender (Summer Only)

From mid-June to early August, the purple fields near Snowshill burst into bloom. Cotswold Lavender Farm offers over 40 varieties of lavender set on a hilltop with views over Broadway and the Vale of Evesham. It's a seasonal spectacle and one of the best sensory experiences in the region.

- **Best for:** Summer travelers, photographers, families
- **Tip:** Visit early in the morning or late afternoon for the best light and fewer crowds.

---

5. Tour Sudeley Castle and Its Award-Winning Gardens

Located near Winchcombe, Sudeley Castle is the only private castle in England with a queen (Katherine Parr, the last wife of Henry VIII) buried on the grounds. The castle boasts over 1,000 years of history and ten separate gardens, including a Tudor parterre and secret garden.

- **Best for:** Garden lovers, families, history aficionados
- **Tip:** Time your visit with seasonal events, like the autumn sculpture trail or spring tulip displays.

---

6. Enjoy a Pub Lunch with a View

The Cotswolds is dotted with traditional pubs set in idyllic landscapes. Favorites include:

- **The Bell at Sapperton** – near the source of the Thames
- **The Wild Rabbit in Kingham** – a modern twist on a countryside classic
- **The Woolpack in Slad** – poet Laurie Lee's old haunt, with valley views

- **Best for:** Foodies, walkers, cultural immersion
- Reserve a table in advance—many of the best countryside pubs now fill up quickly, especially on weekends.

---

7. Visit the Cotswold Wildlife Park and Gardens

Located near Burford, this 160-acre park is home to over 260 animal species, from rhinos to red pandas, all housed in large, landscaped enclosures. The gardens are beautifully maintained, and the setting—on the grounds of a Victorian manor house—adds to its charm.

- **Best for:** Families, animal lovers, day trips
- **Tip:** Arrive early to catch the penguin and lemur feeding sessions, and pack a picnic to enjoy on the lawns.

8. Experience a Traditional Cotswold Market

From weekly farmers' markets to seasonal craft fairs, Cotswold towns come alive with vibrant market culture. Notable markets include:

- **Stroud Farmers' Market (Saturdays)** – award-winning and 100% local
- **Chipping Campden Market Hall** – held under a 17th-century stone arcade
- **Cirencester Charter Market (Mondays & Fridays)** – in the historic market square

- **Best for:** Local culture, foodies, shopping
- **Tip:** Bring cash, as some smaller vendors may not accept cards.

---

9. Tour Hidden Villages by Bike or Car

While villages like Bourton-on-the-Water draw big crowds, smaller gems such as Naunton, Ebrington, Swinbrook, and Eastleach offer quiet lanes, ancient churches, and postcard-perfect scenes without the tourist bustle.

- **Best for:** Repeat visitors, photographers, independent explorers
- **Tip:** Plan a circular driving or cycling route that includes a country pub stop for lunch.

---

10. Stay in a Historic Manor or Thatched Cottage

Accommodations in the Cotswolds are as much a part of the experience as the sights themselves. You can stay in:

- A thatched cottage in Lower Slaughter
- A boutique room in Barnsley House (near Cirencester)
- A restored 17th-century inn like The Lamb Inn in Burford

- **Best for:** Immersion, couples, relaxed travel
- **Tip:** Many of these properties book out months in advance for weekends and holidays—plan ahead.

Chapter 2: Essential Travel Information

When to Visit: Seasonal Guide

The Cotswolds offers year-round beauty, but your experience will vary significantly depending on the season. Here's a detailed breakdown of what to expect in each season, including weather patterns, crowd levels, events, and recommendations to help you choose the best time for your visit.

Spring (March to May)

Best for: Walkers, garden enthusiasts, off-peak travelers

- **Weather:** Mild, with average highs of 10–16°C (50–60°F). Occasional showers, but increasingly sunny days.
- **Landscape:** Meadows come alive with wildflowers, and lambs dot the rolling hills. National Trust gardens and estates reopen for the season.
- **Events:**
    - **Cheltenham Festival (March):** One of Britain's top horse racing events
    - **Tetbury Woolsack Races (late May):** A quirky local event involving competitors running uphill with heavy wool sacks
- **Crowds & Costs:** Fewer tourists and more affordable accommodation than in summer. Perfect for a quiet, scenic holiday.
- **Travel Tip:** Layer your clothing—spring weather can change quickly between sun and showers.

Summer (June to August)

Best for: First-time visitors, families, lavender season, festivals

- **Weather:** Warmest time of year, with average highs of 20–25°C (68–77°F). Occasional heat waves or rainstorms.
- **Landscape:** Peak beauty—lavender fields at Snowshill are in full bloom (mid-June to early August), villages look pristine, and gardens overflow with color.
- **Events:**
    - Cotswold Lavender Season (June–August)
    - **Guiting Music Festival (July):** Classical, jazz, and folk performances in an intimate village setting
    - **Wilderness Festival at Cornbury Park (early August):** Arts, music, and culinary celebration
- **Crowds & Costs:** Peak tourist season. Villages like Bourton-on-the-Water and Bibury can be crowded. Accommodations should be booked 3–6 months in advance.
- **Travel Tip:** Travel early in the morning or late afternoon to avoid crowds at major attractions. Consider visiting lesser-known villages like Naunton or Ebrington for a quieter experience.

Autumn (September to November)

Best for: Food lovers, walkers, scenic photography

- **Weather:** Cooling temperatures, with highs dropping from 18°C (64°F) in September to 8°C (46°F) by November. Misty mornings and crisp air.

- **Landscape:** The Cotswold hills are awash with vibrant autumn colors—gold, amber, and crimson. Harvest season brings farmers' markets and local food festivals.
- **Events:**
  - **Cheltenham Literature Festival (October):** One of the UK's leading literary events
  - **Autumn Colours at Westonbirt Arboretum:** Peak foliage viewing (October)
  - Daylesford Organic Harvest Festival (late September)
- **Crowds & Costs:** Moderate tourism—less busy than summer, but still lively. Accommodation prices drop after mid-October.
- **Travel Tip:** Autumn is ideal for food-focused travel—book a table at one of the Cotswolds' many gastropubs or Michelin-rated inns.

Winter (December to February)

Best for: Cozy getaways, Christmas markets, quiet escapes

- **Weather:** Cold and damp, with average highs of 4–8°C (39–46°F). Occasional snow in higher villages like Snowshill or Winchcombe adds to the charm.
- **Landscape:** Bare trees, frosty mornings, and fireside pub ambience. Villages like Stow-on-the-Wold and Broadway look magical in the snow.
- **Events:**
  - **Christmas Markets:** Cirencester, Cheltenham, and Chipping Campden host atmospheric winter markets with local crafts and mulled wine
  - **Wassailing Ceremonies (January):** Traditional orchard blessings with cider, music, and folklore
- **Crowds & Costs:** Lowest visitor numbers and best accommodation deals. Many attractions operate reduced hours or close entirely, especially in January and February.
- **Travel Tip:** Choose accommodations with fireplaces and on-site dining for a romantic or restful winter escape. Check holiday opening times in advance.

Summary: Best Times by Interest

Interest	Best Time to Visit
Scenic walking & trails	Spring or Autumn

Lavender fields	Mid-June to early August
Cultural events & festivals	Summer
Quiet countryside retreats	Winter
Best weather & gardens	Late Spring (May–June)
Photography & foliage	October

How to Get to the Cotswolds

From London, Oxford, Birmingham, Bristol

The Cotswolds, located in south-central England, is easily accessible from several major cities by car, train, and coach. Here's a detailed guide on how to get there from London, Oxford, Birmingham, and Bristol, covering transport options, travel times, and tips.

From London

By Train

- **Departure stations:** London Paddington or London Marylebone
- **Destination stations:** Moreton-in-Marsh, Kingham, or Kemble (all key gateways to the Cotswolds)
- **Travel time:**
    - **London Paddington to Moreton-in-Marsh:** approx. 1 hour 30 minutes (direct)
    - **London Marylebone to Moreton-in-Marsh:** approx. 2 hours (usually via Oxford or with a change)
- **Frequency:** Around 4-6 trains per day on weekdays from Paddington, slightly fewer on weekends
- **Tickets:** Prices vary; advance purchase recommended for best fares (from £15-£35 one way)
- **Tip:** Moreton-in-Marsh station has a helpful tourist information center and local bus connections.

By Car

- **Route:** M40 motorway out of London, then A40 and A429 into the northern Cotswolds
- **Travel time:** About 2 hours, depending on traffic
- **Considerations:** Driving offers flexibility to explore remote villages and countryside at your own pace, but watch for narrow country lanes and limited parking in villages.

By Coach

- National Express coaches run from London Victoria Coach Station to Cheltenham or Cirencester (major towns near the Cotswolds).
- **Travel time:** Approximately 3 to 4 hours
- **Tip:** Coach is a budget option but less flexible than train or car.

From Oxford

Oxford is the nearest major city to the Cotswolds, making it an ideal gateway.

By Train

- Direct trains from Oxford to Moreton-in-Marsh take about 40 minutes with good frequency throughout the day.
- Alternatively, trains to Kingham take around 30 minutes.
- **Tip:** Oxford station is well connected and easy to reach by bus or taxi from the city center.

By Bus

- The Stagecoach S3 and S4 buses run regularly from Oxford to various Cotswold towns such as Burford, Stow-on-the-Wold, and Bourton-on-the-Water.
- **Travel time:** Typically 1 to 1.5 hours, depending on the town
- **Tip:** Buses are cost-effective and offer a scenic route but check schedules carefully, especially on weekends and holidays.

By Car

- Oxford is just 15-30 minutes' drive from many northern Cotswold villages via the A40 and A44 roads.
- **Tip:** Driving is convenient for day trips or exploring multiple villages.

From Birmingham

Birmingham is located to the north of the Cotswolds, providing good rail and road links.

By Train

- Trains from Birmingham New Street to Moreton-in-Marsh take around 1 hour 45 minutes to 2 hours with typically one change at either Oxford or Worcester.
- Some direct trains may be available but are less frequent.
- **Tip:** Booking in advance can secure cheaper fares, and you'll enjoy countryside views.

By Car

- Take the M42 and M40 motorways southbound, then continue on A40 into the Cotswolds.
- **Travel time:** Around 1.5 to 2 hours depending on traffic.
- **Tip:** Car travel gives you freedom to explore southern and western Cotswold villages less accessible by train.

From Bristol

Bristol lies southwest of the Cotswolds and is a convenient starting point for accessing the western parts of the region.

By Train

- Direct trains from Bristol Temple Meads to Kemble station (gateway to western Cotswolds) take about 45 minutes.
- From Kemble, local buses and taxis connect to Cirencester and other towns.
- **Tip:** Kemble station is smaller, so check train times carefully.

By Car

- The fastest route is via the M4 motorway eastbound, then the A429 north into the Cotswolds.
- **Travel time:** Approximately 1 hour 15 minutes
- **Tip:** Driving allows you to reach less accessible western villages such as Tetbury and Chipping Campden easily.

- National Express coaches run from Bristol to Cirencester, with a travel time of about 2 hours.
- **Tip:** A budget-friendly option, though less flexible and slower than train or car.

By Coach

Summary Table

From	Main Train Station	Approx. Train Time	Approx. Car Time	Coach Option
London	Paddington → Moreton-in-Marsh	1h 30m	~2 hours	Yes, to Cheltenham/Cirencester
Oxford	Oxford → Moreton-in-Marsh	40 minutes	15–30 mins	Yes, buses to towns
Birmingham	Birmingham New Street → Moreton-in-Marsh	1h 45m–2h	1.5–2 hours	Limited
Bristol	Bristol Temple Meads → Kemble	45 minutes	1h 15m	Yes, to Cirencester

International Airports & Transfers to the Cotswolds

Primary International Airports Serving the Cotswolds

The Cotswolds, while a largely rural and historic region, is well connected internationally via several major airports within convenient reach. Visitors typically fly into one of these airports and then transfer to the Cotswolds by train, coach, or car.

---

1. London Heathrow Airport (LHR)

- **Location:** 25 miles west of central London
- **Distance to Cotswolds:** Approximately 75 miles (120 km) to northern Cotswolds towns such as Moreton-in-Marsh or Chipping Norton
- **Transfers:**
    - **By Train:** Take the Heathrow Express or Elizabeth Line to London Paddington (15–25 minutes), then a direct train to Moreton-in-Marsh (1h 30m). Total transfer time approx. 2 to 2.5 hours.
    - **By Car:** Rental cars are widely available. Drive via M40 motorway; journey time roughly 1.5 to 2 hours depending on traffic.
    - **By Coach:** National Express and other operators run services from Heathrow to Cheltenham or Cirencester, with transfer times around 3 to 4 hours including connections.

---

2. Birmingham Airport (BHX)

- **Location:** Approximately 7 miles east of Birmingham city center
- **Distance to Cotswolds:** About 40 miles (65 km) to northern Cotswolds towns such as Moreton-in-Marsh and Broadway
- **Transfers:**
    - **By Train:** From Birmingham International railway station (connected directly to the airport), take trains to Moreton-in-Marsh (1h 45m to 2h, usually via Birmingham New Street and Oxford).
    - **By Car:** Driving via the M42 and M40 motorways takes approximately 1.5 hours.
    - **Coach:** Less frequent; possible but generally slower and less convenient.

---

3. Bristol Airport (BRS)

- **Location:** About 8 miles south of Bristol city center
- **Distance to Cotswolds:** Around 40 miles (65 km) to southwestern towns such as Cirencester and Tetbury
- **Transfers:**
    - **By Train:** No direct train from airport, but shuttle bus available to Bristol Temple Meads station (30 minutes), then train to Kemble (approx. 45 minutes), and onward bus or taxi into the Cotswolds.
    - **By Car:** Rental cars are convenient; drive via M4 and A429 to Cirencester in about 1 hour 15 minutes.
    - **Coach:** National Express coaches operate between Bristol and Cirencester; travel time approx. 2 hours.

4. London Gatwick Airport (LGW)

- **Location:** 30 miles south of London
- **Distance to Cotswolds:** About 100 miles (160 km) to the Cotswolds
- **Transfers:**
    - **By Train:** Take Gatwick Express or Southern Rail to London Victoria, then underground to Paddington or Marylebone, followed by train to Moreton-in-Marsh. Total journey time approx. 3.5 to 4 hours.
    - **By Car:** Driving via M25 and M40 takes approximately 2.5 to 3 hours depending on traffic.
    - **Coach:** Longer and less convenient, not generally recommended.

5. London Stansted Airport (STN)

- **Location:** 40 miles northeast of London
- **Distance to Cotswolds:** Roughly 110 miles (175 km)
- **Transfers:**
    - **By Train:** Stansted Express to London Liverpool Street (~45 minutes), then London underground to Paddington or Marylebone, then train to the Cotswolds. Total travel time 3.5 to 4 hours.
    - **By Car:** Driving via M25 and M40, around 2.5 to 3 hours.
    - **Coach:** Long and indirect; not typically recommended.

Airport Transfer Tips

- **Advance Bookings:** For peace of mind, pre-book train tickets and airport transfers where possible, especially during peak travel seasons.
- **Car Rentals:** Rental cars are available at all major airports and offer the greatest flexibility for exploring the Cotswolds, particularly for remote villages with limited public transport.
- **Taxi Services:** Taxis and private transfers can be booked in advance, but are considerably more expensive than public transport or car hire.
- **Public Transport Apps:** Use apps like National Rail Enquiries and Traveline for real-time train and bus information.
- **Luggage:** If arriving by train, check if your connecting services have luggage assistance or storage facilities, especially for trips involving multiple changes.

Summary Table: Airport to Cotswolds Approximate Transfer Times

Airport	Nearest Cotswolds Gateway	Transfer Options	Approx. Transfer Time
London Heathrow	Moreton-in-Marsh	Train, Car, Coach	2–2.5 hours (train), 1.5–2 hrs (car)

Birmingham	Moreton-in-Marsh	Train, Car	1.75–2 hours (train), 1.5 hrs (car)
Bristol	Cirencester / Kemble	Shuttle + Train, Car	1.5–2 hours
London Gatwick	Moreton-in-Marsh	Train, Car	3.5–4 hours
London Stansted	Moreton-in-Marsh	Train, Car	3.5–4 hours

Getting Around the Cotswolds

The Cotswolds is a picturesque rural region of rolling hills, quaint villages, and country lanes, meaning transportation options vary widely in convenience and availability. While the region has a charmingly traditional feel, modern transport connections are good but somewhat limited outside the main towns. Here's a comprehensive guide to moving around:

Car Hire

By far the most flexible and popular way to explore the Cotswolds is by renting a car. The area's many narrow, winding country roads and small villages are best experienced at your own pace, without worrying about bus or train timetables.

- **Where to rent:** Major international airports (Heathrow, Birmingham, Bristol) and larger towns such as Oxford, Cheltenham, and Gloucester all have multiple rental agencies including Avis, Enterprise, Hertz, and Sixt.

- **Cost:** Expect to pay approximately £35–£60 per day for a small to mid-sized car; prices may increase in peak seasons (spring and summer) and during weekends. Fuel costs are roughly £1.50–£1.70 per litre (2025 estimates).

- **Driving conditions:** Roads are often narrow with occasional single-track sections, so a smaller car is advisable. Parking in villages like Bourton-on-the-Water, Stow-on-the-Wold, and Chipping Campden is limited but usually available in public car parks with daily charges from £3 to £6.

- **Tips:** Some villages restrict vehicle access during peak times to preserve the environment. Always check local signage, and be cautious on rural roads with cyclists, pedestrians, and farm vehicles.

Trains

The Cotswolds has several key train stations linking it to major cities, ideal for travelers who prefer not to drive.

- **Main stations:** Moreton-in-Marsh, Kingham, and Kemble are the primary rail gateways to the Cotswolds.

- **Routes:**
    - From London Paddington, trains run directly to Moreton-in-Marsh in about 1 hour 30 minutes, costing between £20 and £40 one-way depending on booking time and class.

- From Oxford, direct trains to Moreton-in-Marsh take around 40 minutes with fares from £10 to £15.
- From Bristol Temple Meads, a 45-minute journey to Kemble costs about £12 to £18.

- **Limitations:** Most Cotswold villages are not directly served by trains, so onward transport (bus, taxi) from the station is needed. Train services are generally frequent on weekdays but more limited on Sundays.

Buses

Public bus service is the most affordable but least frequent way to get around the Cotswolds, suitable mainly for those staying in or visiting larger towns.

- **Operators:** Stagecoach West runs most routes connecting Oxford, Cheltenham, Cirencester, Moreton-in-Marsh, and towns such as Bourton-on-the-Water, Stow-on-the-Wold, and Chipping Campden.

- **Typical routes:**
  - The S3 bus runs between Oxford and Stow-on-the-Wold via Burford and Bourton-on-the-Water.
  - Route 801 links Cirencester to Cheltenham and Tetbury.

- **Costs:** Single fares typically range from £3 to £6 depending on distance. Day passes are often available for £8–£12, offering flexibility.

- **Frequency:** Buses usually run every 1-2 hours on weekdays but can be sparse or non-existent on Sundays and public holidays. Evening services are limited.

- **Tips:** Always check current timetables in advance, as routes and frequencies can change seasonally. Bus travel provides scenic views but requires some patience.

Taxis and Private Transfers

Taxis are available in the main towns but are relatively expensive compared to public transport.

- **Availability:** Most towns have local taxi companies that can be booked by phone or app, but wait times can be long in rural areas without advance notice.

- **Cost:** Typical fares from a train station to a nearby village run between £10 and £25 for short trips (3–6 miles). Longer journeys (20+ miles) can easily exceed £50–£70. Pre-booking private transfers or minibuses can offer a fixed price for group travel.

- **Tips:** If arriving by train or coach, arrange a taxi in advance for convenience.

Walking and Cycling

Many visitors relish exploring the Cotswolds on foot or by bike, with a vast network of footpaths and cycle routes.

- **Walking:** The Cotswolds is famed for the Cotswold Way National Trail, a 102-mile route running from Chipping Campden in the north to Bath in the south. Daily walking sections vary in difficulty and length, with well-marked trails through fields, woodland, and villages.

- **Costs:** Free aside from possible parking or accommodation.

- **Cycling:** Numerous scenic cycling routes cover the region, including relatively flat lanes suited for casual cyclists and hillier terrain for enthusiasts. Bike hire shops are located in towns like Cirencester, Cheltenham, and Chipping Campden, charging around £15–£25 per day for a standard bike.

- **Tips:** Public rights of way allow for varied exploration, but be mindful of private land boundaries and livestock.

Summary

- For maximum freedom and flexibility, renting a car is the best choice, especially if you want to visit multiple villages or off-the-beaten-path sites.
- Use trains for fast, comfortable access to main towns and combine with local taxis or buses.
- Buses are economical but limited in coverage and frequency; ideal for travelers on a budget or staying in major towns.
- Taxis offer convenience for short distances but can be costly; pre-booking is recommended.
- Walking and cycling offer immersive experiences of the Cotswolds' natural beauty and are great for those wanting an active holiday.

Where to Stay: Accommodation Guide

The Cotswolds offers a charming range of accommodations that perfectly complement its pastoral beauty and historic ambiance. Whether you're seeking luxury, rustic charm, or a cozy countryside retreat, the region's lodging options deliver unforgettable experiences. Having explored many of these myself, here's a breakdown of the best types of places to stay, what makes each special, and practical info on costs.

Boutique Hotels

If you want style and personalized service combined with Cotswolds character, boutique hotels are the ideal choice. These properties often blend historic architecture with contemporary design and offer excellent dining and spa facilities.

- **Why stay here:** Boutique hotels provide a refined yet intimate atmosphere. Expect beautifully decorated rooms with local touches—think exposed beams, antique furnishings, and modern comforts like underfloor heating and luxury toiletries. They often have award-winning restaurants showcasing seasonal, locally sourced ingredients, so dining is an experience itself.

- **Recommended:**
    - **The Lygon Arms (Broadway):** A historic coaching inn dating back to the 1300s, recently refurbished with elegant rooms, a spa, and a Michelin-starred restaurant. Staying here immerses you in centuries of history while enjoying modern luxury.
    - **Ellenborough Park (Cheltenham):** A manor house hotel with a chic, contemporary feel and top-notch spa facilities. Perfect for blending Cotswold charm with wellness relaxation.

- **Typical costs:** Expect to pay from £150 to £350 per night for a double room, with suites going higher during peak season. Weekend rates and special event weekends (like Cheltenham Festival) can push prices up.

Countryside Inns

For a quintessential English country experience, nothing beats staying in a traditional countryside inn. These are often family-run, with cozy rooms, open fires, and a lively pub atmosphere serving classic British fare.

- **Why stay here:** Countryside inns offer warmth, friendliness, and easy access to village life. They are perfect if you want to mix local culture with convenience and hearty food. Many inns have charming gardens and provide walking maps for nearby trails.

- **Recommended:**
    - **The Fleece Inn (Broadway):** A beloved timber-framed 15th-century pub and inn that's cozy and authentic, offering comfy rooms and exceptional pub food. The atmosphere feels like stepping back in time with a welcoming community vibe.
    - **The Wild Rabbit (Kingham):** A Michelin-starred gastropub with a few rooms upstairs. The food is superb, and the village setting makes it a perfect base for exploring.

- **Typical costs:** Rooms here generally range from £90 to £160 per night. Booking in advance is recommended as these popular inns fill quickly, especially during tourist season.

Manor Houses

For a truly grand and historic stay, the Cotswolds' manor houses are a dream. These large country estates often date back centuries and have been lovingly preserved or restored as luxury hotels or private rentals.

- **Why stay here:** Manor houses combine stately elegance, sprawling gardens, and an authentic sense of English heritage. Many feature period furnishings, extensive grounds for walking, and in some cases, access to private hunting lodges or gardens. Staying here feels like living in a Jane Austen novel.

- **Recommended:**
    - **Barnsley House (Cirencester):** A stunning

manor with award-winning gardens designed by Rosemary Verey, combined with luxurious rooms and a celebrated spa. The onsite restaurant features locally grown produce.

- **Dormy House (Broadway):** An elegant 17th-century manor turned boutique hotel with excellent amenities, including a pool and spa. It's both relaxing and picturesque.

- **Typical costs:** Manor house stays tend to be premium, with rooms typically starting around £250 and reaching £500+ per night. Off-peak rates and midweek stays offer better value.

Cottages

For an intimate, private, and homey experience, renting a traditional Cotswold stone cottage is unbeatable. Whether a romantic hideaway or a family base, cottages offer self-catering flexibility and a strong connection to local life.

- **Why stay here:** Cottages let you live like a local with cozy fireplaces, rustic kitchens, and quiet gardens. Many are located in idyllic villages like Bibury, Painswick, or Upper Slaughter, where mornings feel like a painting come to life. They're perfect for those who value privacy, slow mornings, and cooking with fresh local produce.

- **Recommended:**
  - **Bibury Cottages:** Numerous stone cottages available, many dating back to the 17th century, featuring exposed beams, thatched roofs, and flower-filled gardens. Perfect for couples or small groups.
  - **The Old Bakery (Stow-on-the-Wold):** A beautifully restored historic cottage with modern comforts, right in the heart of town for easy access to shops and pubs.

- **Typical costs:** Depending on size and location, cottage rentals typically start at £100 per night for small 1-2 bedroom properties and can rise to £300+ for larger, more luxurious options. Weekly rentals often come with discounts.

Summary

- Choose boutique hotels if you want luxury, style, and top-notch dining/spa experiences.
- Opt for countryside inns for authentic local hospitality and cozy pub culture.
- Stay in a manor house for grandeur, history, and exquisite gardens.
- Rent a cottage for privacy, self-catering, and the purest village atmosphere.

Whichever you pick, booking early is essential—especially for the high season between May and September, or during events like the Cheltenham Festival and Cotswolds Literary Festival.

Budgeting Your Trip: Costs & Money Tips

Traveling to the Cotswolds offers a range of budget options, from luxury manor houses to modest inns and self-catering cottages. To help you plan realistically, here's a detailed breakdown of typical costs you can expect and smart money-saving tips to maximize your experience without overspending.

Typical Costs Breakdown

Accommodation:

- **Budget options (guesthouses, inns, some cottages):** £70–£120 per night
- **Mid-range boutique hotels and well-appointed cottages:** £130–£250 per night
- **Luxury manor houses and upscale boutique hotels:** £250–£500+ per night

Food & Drink:

- **Casual pubs and cafés:** £10–£20 for a meal
- **Mid-range restaurants:** £25–£45 per person for a three-course meal
- **Fine dining (Michelin-starred or gourmet country house restaurants):** £60–£100+ per person
- **Groceries (for self-catering):** £25–£40 per day depending on your preferences

Transport:

- **Car hire:** £35–£60 per day, plus fuel (£1.50–£1.70 per litre)
- **Train fares (London to Moreton-in-Marsh):** £20–£40 one-way
- **Local buses:** £3–£6 per journey, day passes around £8–£12
- **Taxi rides:** £10–£25 for short trips, £50+ for longer transfers

Attractions & Activities:

- **Entry fees to gardens and historic houses:** £10–£20 per person
- **Guided tours (walking or cycling):** £15–£40 per person
- **Special experiences (hot air balloon rides, spa days):** £80–£200+

Money-Saving Tips

1. Book Accommodation Early:

The Cotswolds is a popular destination year-round, especially in spring and summer. Booking your lodging 3–6 months in advance often secures the best rates and availability, especially for boutique hotels and manor houses.

2. Consider Self-Catering:

Renting a cottage or staying in accommodation with kitchen facilities allows you to save on dining out by preparing some meals yourself, especially breakfast and light lunches. Local markets and farm shops provide fresh, affordable ingredients.

3. Use Railcards and Advance Train Tickets:

If traveling by train, purchase a railcard (e.g., the 16-25 Railcard, Senior Railcard, or Two Together Railcard) to save up to 1/3 on fares. Booking train tickets in advance (usually 12 weeks ahead) can reduce costs significantly.

4. Opt for Regional Buses:

While slower and less frequent, buses are an economical way to move between towns and villages. Look for day passes or multi-ride tickets for better value.

5. Take Advantage of Free Attractions:

Many Cotswold villages and natural sights, such as walking the Cotswold Way or visiting village greens and churches, are free. Plan your itinerary to balance paid attractions with these budget-friendly options.

6. Travel Off-Peak:

Visiting during shoulder seasons (late autumn, winter, early spring) can reduce accommodation and transport costs substantially. Many places offer off-season discounts, and the area is less crowded.

7. Use Local Pubs and Cafés for Meals:

Eating in traditional pubs or local cafés often provides generous portions at lower prices than tourist-focused restaurants. Try daily specials or set menus for good value.

8. Limit Taxi Use:

Taxi fares in rural areas add up quickly. Use them sparingly or for essential transfers, and consider booking private transfers in advance to lock in prices.

Practical Tips for Handling Money

- **Currency:** The Cotswolds uses British Pounds (£). Credit and debit cards are widely accepted, but always carry some cash, especially in smaller villages or at local markets.

- **ATMs:** Available in larger towns such as Cirencester, Moreton-in-Marsh, and Stow-on-the-Wold. Some small villages may lack cash machines, so plan accordingly.

- **Tipping:** Tipping around 10–15% in restaurants and cafés is customary if service is good. For taxis, rounding up the fare or adding a small tip is appreciated but not mandatory.

- **Currency Exchange:** If arriving from abroad, exchange some currency before traveling or withdraw cash at local ATMs for better rates. Avoid airport exchanges, which tend to have poor rates.

Summary

A Cotswolds trip can be tailored to fit most budgets, from frugal travelers relying on inns and buses to those indulging in luxury stays and fine dining. Early planning and a mix of self-catering, public transport, and selective splurges will stretch your pounds further without sacrificing experience. Always check current prices and availability ahead of your visit to avoid surprises.

3 and 7-Day Budgeting Plans for Travellers

3-Day Budget Trip to the Cotswolds

Day 1: Arrival and Exploring a Cotswold Town

- **Accommodation:**
  Book a budget-friendly inn or guesthouse in a town like Moreton-in-Marsh or Stow-on-the-Wold. Expect around £70–£90 per night for a simple double room with basic amenities. Booking through Airbnb or local B&B websites can sometimes offer even better deals.

- **Transportation:**
  Take a train from London Paddington to Moreton-in-Marsh — advance tickets can cost £15–£25 one way with an off-peak fare. From the station, walk or take a local bus (about £3) to your accommodation.

- **Meals:**
  - For breakfast, buy pastries and coffee from a local bakery (£5).
  - **Lunch:** Enjoy a pub lunch with a sandwich and drink for around £10.
  - **Dinner:** Pick a local pub offering a daily special or set menu, approximately £15.

- **Activities:**
  - Spend the afternoon exploring the town's market square and local shops — free to stroll. Visit the Moreton-in-Marsh Heritage Centre for about £5 entry.

- Evening walk along the nearby Cotswold Way — free.

- **Daily Total Estimate:**
  - Accommodation £80 + Transport £25 + Food £30 + Activities £5 = £140

Day 2: Villages and Countryside Walks

- **Accommodation:** Same as Day 1, no extra cost.

- **Transportation:**

  Use local buses or rent a bike for the day (~£15). Bus day pass around £8–£10 if available. Walking is free and highly recommended between villages like Bourton-on-the-Water and Upper Slaughter.

- **Meals:**
  - **Breakfast:** Provided at accommodation or light shop-bought (£5).
  - **Lunch:** Picnic from local grocery shop for £8 (sandwiches, fruit, snacks).
  - **Dinner:** Budget pub meal or takeaway fish and chips for around £12.

- **Activities:**
  - Visit Bourton-on-the-Water Model Village (£6 entry).
  - Walk through Upper and Lower Slaughter villages (free).
  - Explore Cotswold Motoring Museum (£7).

- **Daily Total Estimate:**
  - Accommodation £80 + Transport £15 + Food £25 + Activities £13 = £133

Day 3: Historic Houses & Departure

- **Accommodation:** None (checking out).

- **Transportation:**

  Bus or taxi to a nearby historic site like Sudeley Castle (~£6 bus or £15 taxi). Return train from Moreton-in-Marsh to London approx. £20–£30.

- **Meals:**
  - **Breakfast:** Provided for £5 from a bakery.
  - **Lunch:** Light pub meal or café snack £10.
  - Snacks for journey £3.

- **Activities:**
  - Visit Sudeley Castle & Gardens (£15 entry).

- **Daily Total Estimate:**
  - Transport £45 + Food £18 + Activities £15 = £78

3-Day Trip Total Budget:

£140 + £133 + £78 = £351

7-Day Budget Trip to the Cotswolds

Days 1-3:

Follow the same plan as above for Days 1–3. Total =

£351

Day 4: Day Trip to Cirencester

- **Accommodation:** Same budget inn or B&B (£70–£90).
- **Transportation:**
  - Bus or local train to Cirencester (£5–£8 round trip).
- **Meals:**
  - **Breakfast:** Included or £5 shop-bought.
  - **Lunch:** Pub meal in Cirencester, £12.
  - **Dinner:** Simple takeaway or café meal, £10.
- **Activities:**
  - Visit Corinium Museum (free or donation-based).
  - Walk around Cirencester Park (free).
- **Daily Total Estimate:**
  - Accommodation £80 + Transport £8 + Food £27 + Activities £0 = £115

Day 5: Explore Broadway & Nearby Villages

- **Accommodation:** Same (£70–£90).
- **Transportation:**
  - Bus or bike hire (£10–£15).
- **Meals:**
  - **Breakfast:** £5.
  - **Lunch:** Picnic from local shops, £8.
  - **Dinner:** Budget-friendly pub meal, £12.
- **Activities:**
  - Walk Broadway Tower grounds (£8 entry).
  - Explore villages on foot or bike (free).
- **Daily Total Estimate:**
  - Accommodation £80 + Transport £12 + Food £25 + Activities £8 = £125

Day 6: Relaxed Day with Free Activities

- **Accommodation:** Same (£70–£90).
- **Transportation:**
  - Mostly walking or local bus (£5).
- **Meals:**
  - **Breakfast:** Included or £5.
  - **Lunch:** Sandwiches/picnic from market, £8.
  - **Dinner:** Simple meal at local café or pub, £12.
- **Activities:**
  - Walking the Cotswold Way or visiting village greens and churches (free).
  - Visit local markets or craft shops (window shopping/free).
- **Daily Total Estimate:**
  - Accommodation £80 + Transport £5 + Food £25 + Activities £0 = £110

Day 7: Departure Day

- **Accommodation:** None (checkout).
- **Transportation:**
  - Train or bus back to London or next destination, £20–£30.

- **Meals:**
    - **Breakfast:** £5.
    - **Lunch:** £10.
    - **Snacks:** £3.

- **Activities:**
    - None planned.

- Daily Total Estimate:
    - Transport £25 + Food £18 = £43

7-Day Trip Total Budget:

- **Days 1-3:** £351
- **Day 4:** £115
- **Day 5:** £125
- **Day 6:** £110
- **Day 7:** £43

Grand total: £744

Additional Money-Saving Tips for Both Plans

- Book trains early for best fares.
- Use local grocery shops for picnic supplies rather than eating out all the time.
- Walk as much as possible to save on transport and soak in the scenery.
- Check for free museum days or discounted entry passes online.
- Stay in the same accommodation for multiple nights to avoid extra check-in fees or transport costs.

Local Etiquette & Safety

Visiting the Cotswolds offers a charming experience steeped in English rural traditions and hospitality. To fully enjoy your trip while showing respect to locals and ensuring your safety, it's important to be aware of local etiquette and common safety practices.

Local Etiquette

1. Politeness and Courtesy

The English countryside is known for its polite and reserved culture. When interacting with locals—whether shopkeepers, pub staff, or residents—use polite greetings such as "Good morning" or "Hello." Saying "Please" and "Thank you" goes a long way in making a positive impression.

2. Queuing

The British are famously orderly about queuing. Whether at the bus stop, shops, or pubs, always wait your turn patiently in line. Cutting in or pushing ahead is considered very rude.

3. Pub Behavior

Pubs are social hubs in the Cotswolds, but local customs should be followed:

- It's common to order drinks at the bar rather than waiting for table service.
- Avoid raising your voice excessively; keep conversations polite and friendly.
- When buying rounds for friends, wait until everyone has finished before ordering the next.
- Tipping around 10% is appreciated but not mandatory.

4. Respect for Private Property

Many parts of the Cotswolds countryside are privately owned farmland or gardens. Always stick to public footpaths and trails, and never trespass on private land without permission. When walking dogs, keep them under control and clear up after them.

5. Environment and Waste

The Cotswolds prides itself on clean villages and natural beauty. Dispose of litter responsibly in bins or carry it with you if none are available. Avoid disturbing wildlife or picking flowers in protected areas.

6. Photography

It's generally fine to take photos of public areas and scenic spots, but be respectful if you are photographing people or private properties. Always ask permission if unsure.

Safety Tips

1. General Safety

The Cotswolds is one of the safest regions in England, with low crime rates. However, as in any tourist area, keep an eye on your belongings in crowded places and avoid leaving valuables unattended in vehicles.

2. Road Safety

If driving, remember the UK drives on the left side of the road. Many rural roads are narrow and winding, so drive cautiously and be prepared to give way at passing points. Watch for pedestrians, cyclists, and farm vehicles.

3. Walking and Hiking Safety

- Stick to marked trails, especially when walking the Cotswold Way or other long-distance paths.
- Wear suitable footwear as paths can be muddy or uneven, especially in wet weather.
- Check the weather forecast before heading out and dress in layers.
- Carry water, a map (physical or downloaded offline), and a fully charged phone.
- Inform someone of your route if walking alone.

4. Emergency Services

- For any emergency requiring police, fire, or medical assistance, dial 999 in the UK.
- For non-emergency police matters, use 101.
- Most villages have local GP surgeries or pharmacies for minor health issues. Larger towns such as Cirencester and Moreton-in-Marsh have medical centers and hospitals.

5. COVID-19 Considerations (as of 2025/2026)

While restrictions have largely eased, it's advisable to stay updated on any local health guidelines. Carry hand sanitizer and wear masks in crowded indoor spaces if you prefer. Check policies at accommodations and attractions before visiting.

Summary

Showing respect through politeness, understanding local customs, and adhering to safety advice will ensure a smooth and enjoyable trip in the Cotswolds. The locals appreciate visitors who honor the peaceful rural lifestyle and natural environment, and your awareness will contribute to a positive travel experience for all.

Language & Communication Tips

1. English in the Cotswolds

The primary language spoken is English, with a distinctive regional accent known as the West Country or Cotswold accent. While most locals speak clear English, some village residents may use traditional expressions or local dialect words. Don't hesitate to ask for clarification if you don't understand something.

2. Politeness Matters

British English favors polite expressions and indirect phrasing. Common courtesy phrases like "please," "thank you," and "excuse me" are expected and appreciated. Even small efforts in politeness make a positive impression.

3. Pace and Volume

Speak clearly and at a moderate pace. Avoid speaking too loudly; the British typically use a softer tone in everyday conversation.

4. Understanding Local Terms

Some traditional or local terms may come up, especially in rural settings. For example:

- "Loo" means toilet/restroom.
- "Pub" refers to a local bar or inn.
- "Biscuit" means cookie.
- "Cheers" is often used to mean thanks or goodbye.
- "Brilliant" means excellent or great.

Basic English Phrases for Travelers

Purpose	Phrase	Notes
Greetings	Hello / Good morning / Good evening	Simple and polite greetings.
Polite Requests	Please / Could you help me? / Excuse me	Use these when asking for help or directions.
Thanking Someone	Thank you / Thanks very much	Always appreciated.
Asking Directions	Where is the nearest bus stop? / How do I get to the train station?	Useful when navigating.
Shopping & Dining	How much is this? / Can I have the menu, please? / Is service included?	Helpful in markets and restaurants.
Emergencies	I need help / Call the police / Is there a doctor nearby?	Important for urgent situations.

General Help	Could you please repeat that? / I don't understand / Do you speak [your language]?	Useful when there's a language barrier.
Farewells	Goodbye / See you later / Have a nice day	Polite endings to conversations.

Additional Tips

- **Listening:** Pay attention to tone and context; British English often uses understatement and humor.
- **Writing:** When filling forms or booking, use clear, simple English.
- **Using Technology:** Most places have good mobile coverage and Wi-Fi, so translation apps can assist when needed.
- **Local Newspapers and Signs:** Usually in standard English and helpful for learning common phrases or terms.

Chapter 3: Regions & Villages Of The Cotswolds

Overview of Cotswolds Geography & Layout

Having spent significant time wandering through the Cotswolds, I can say this region is far more than just a pretty collection of villages. It's a vast and varied landscape that stretches across six counties, creating one of England's most beloved Areas of Outstanding Natural Beauty (AONB). To truly appreciate its charm and plan your trip wisely, it helps to understand the geography and how the region is laid out.

The Physical Landscape

At its core, the Cotswolds is defined by a series of gently rolling limestone hills, formed from the Jurassic-era sedimentary rock known as Cotswold stone. This golden-hued limestone not only shapes the geology but also gives the region's villages and buildings their signature warm glow. The hills reach their highest point at Cleeve Hill near Cheltenham, which peaks at about 330 meters (1,083 feet).

Between these hills lie peaceful valleys and meadows dotted with ancient dry stone walls, pasture lands, and wooded areas. Small rivers such as the Windrush, Evenlode, and Leach weave through these valleys, enhancing the pastoral charm and providing perfect spots for riverside walks.

The Regional Layout

The Cotswolds stretch in a broad arc roughly 80 miles long, from the city of Bath in the southwest up to the historic town of Stratford-upon-Avon in the northeast. It covers parts of Gloucestershire, Oxfordshire, Warwickshire, Wiltshire, Worcestershire, and Somerset, though Gloucestershire and Oxfordshire contain the heart of what most visitors imagine as the Cotswolds.

Visitors often think of the Cotswolds as a single destination, but it's really a mosaic of smaller regions and clusters of villages, each with its own character:

- **Southern Cotswolds:** This area feels gently pastoral with a mix of charming villages like Castle Combe and Tetbury. It's quieter and less touristy, with beautiful stately homes such as Highgrove (the Prince of Wales' residence) and rich farming landscapes.

- **Central Cotswolds:** This is where the iconic Cotswolds villages thrive. Places like Bourton-on-the-Water, with its quaint low bridges over the River Windrush, and Stow-on-the-Wold, a bustling market town with antiques shops, pubs, and a large central square, offer that classic picture-postcard experience.

- **Northern Cotswolds:** Bordering the Cotswold Edge escarpment, this region is slightly more elevated and rugged. Towns like Chipping Campden and Moreton-in-Marsh are well-known hubs with historical wool markets and vibrant local culture. This area is also the start point for the Cotswold Way, a 102-mile walking trail running along the ridgeline of the hills.

Accessibility and Travel Flow

Because the Cotswolds consists of many small, dispersed villages connected by narrow country roads, getting around can feel like stepping back in time. Roads wind around hills and fields, and travel is as much about the journey as the destination. While train stations at Moreton-in-Marsh, Kingham, and Kemble offer entry points, most visitors find having a car essential for exploring beyond the main hubs.

The layout encourages a slow-paced itinerary — you'll find yourself lingering at a village café or stopping to photograph an ancient church or a stack of dry stone walls.

Why Geography Matters to Your Visit

The distinct geography of the Cotswolds shapes every visitor experience. The hills provide breathtaking panoramic views, while the sheltered valleys feel intimate and timeless. Understanding where these areas lie will help you plan visits according to your interests — whether you're chasing the quintessential village scene, hiking rugged trails, or exploring historic market towns.

By grasping this geographic layout, you'll uncover the Cotswolds' layers of history, culture, and natural beauty with more insight and ease.

Northern Cotswolds Highlights

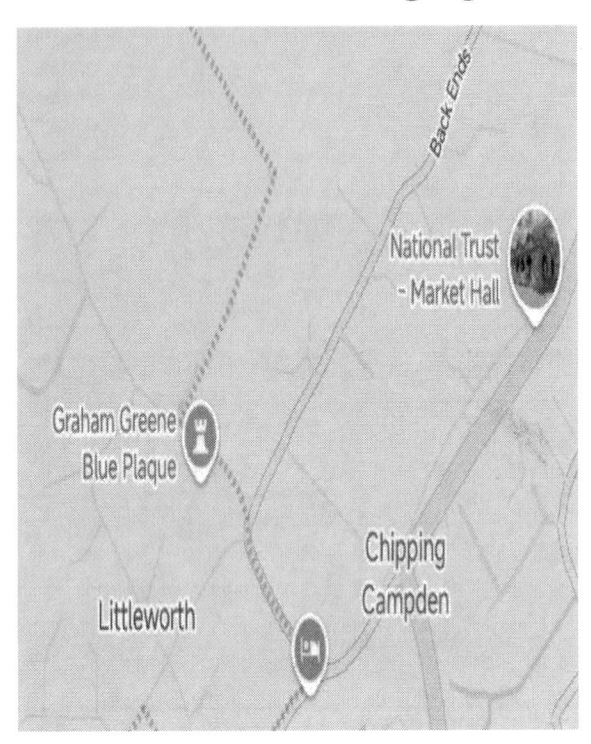

Chipping Campden

Chipping Campden stands as one of the crown jewels of the Northern Cotswolds, a quintessential English market town that perfectly balances historic charm with a vibrant cultural scene. I've visited Chipping Campden on multiple occasions, and each time I'm struck by how it manages to feel timeless yet lively—this is a place that draws visitors not just for its postcard-perfect stone buildings, but for its rich heritage and genuinely welcoming community.

Located in Gloucestershire, about 22 miles northeast of Cheltenham and roughly 110 miles west of London, Chipping Campden is easily accessible by car or train (nearest station: Moreton-in-Marsh, about 6 miles away, with regular direct trains from London Paddington taking around 1 hour 45 minutes). For travelers on a budget, a return train ticket from London can range between £25-£45 if booked in advance, making it a feasible day-trip destination or an overnight stay.

The town's origins as a prosperous wool-trading center are visible in its architecture: the wide High Street is lined with beautifully preserved limestone buildings dating back to the 14th and 15th centuries. Walking down this street feels like stepping into history, with its medieval market hall — a focal point dating from 1627 — serving as a reminder of the town's mercantile past. The term "Chipping" means market, and the traditional market still operates weekly on Saturdays, where you can find local crafts, fresh produce, and artisan goods. It's a fantastic way to soak up the local atmosphere without any touristy gloss.

Why visit Chipping Campden? Beyond the obvious aesthetic appeal, it's a cultural hub within the Cotswolds. The town was a key center for the Arts and Crafts Movement in the early 20th century, attracting notable figures such as architect C.R. Ashbee and craftsmen like Ernest Gimson. Today, you can explore numerous galleries, studios, and craft shops that keep this tradition alive. Visiting the Court Barn Museum gives a deeper understanding of this artistic heritage, with exhibitions focusing on local crafts and history; entry costs about £5 and it's well worth the visit.

Food-wise, Chipping Campden offers a variety of options from traditional pubs like The Eight Bells — a charming 17th-century inn known for excellent local ales and hearty meals (main courses typically £15-£25) — to fine dining at the Michelin-starred Dormy House nearby, for those looking to indulge.

If you're into walking, Chipping Campden is the start (or finish) of the famous Cotswold Way National Trail, a 102-mile footpath running along the Cotswold Edge escarpment. From here, you can embark on shorter hikes with stunning views over the Warwickshire countryside, perfect for a half-day outing. Maps and guides for these walks are available locally and cost around £3-£5.

Accommodation ranges from quaint bed and breakfasts starting at around £80 per night in low season, to boutique hotels and historic inns costing upwards of £150 per night. Booking in advance is recommended, especially during spring and summer when the town hosts the annual Cotswold Olimpicks — a unique traditional sporting event dating back to the early 1600s, which draws visitors from across the country.

Practical tip: Parking in the town center can be limited, so if you're driving, use one of the public car parks on the outskirts (£3-£5 per day) and enjoy a short walk into the heart of town.

In sum, Chipping Campden isn't just a pretty stop on the tourist trail — it's a living community rich in history, craft, and culture. Whether you're there for a day or a few nights, it offers a genuine slice of Cotswold life that's both accessible and deeply rewarding.

Broadway

Broadway, often referred to as the "Jewel of the Cotswolds," is a village that embodies everything charming and idyllic about this region, making it a must-visit destination in the Northern Cotswolds. Nestled in Worcestershire, about 18 miles northeast of Cheltenham and roughly 110 miles northwest of London, Broadway is easily accessible by car via the A44, which links Oxford to Worcester. If relying on public transport, the closest railway station is at Honeybourne, about 5 miles away, but services are limited; therefore, a car is highly recommended for flexibility and ease.

What sets Broadway apart is its striking high street lined with perfectly preserved honey-colored limestone buildings that date back to the 16th and 17th centuries. This street is wide and inviting, flanked by boutique shops, art galleries, and cozy cafés that create a warm, village atmosphere while still offering a touch of sophistication. The village has attracted visitors for centuries, including artists and writers, partly because of its serene beauty and partly due to its historical importance as a coaching stop on the old route between London and Worcester.

Why go to Broadway? First, it's the quintessential Cotswolds experience — the architecture, the peaceful village greens, and the picturesque backdrop of the rolling countryside are all postcard-perfect. Broadway Tower, just a mile outside the village, is a highlight: a unique folly built in 1798 standing on Broadway Hill, the second highest point in the Cotswolds at 1,024 feet. The tower offers panoramic views over 16 counties on a clear day. Entry costs about £7.50 for adults and includes access to the surrounding parkland where you can spot deer and enjoy scenic walking trails. The tower café is an excellent spot to rest and soak in the views.

Food and drink options on Broadway are excellent and varied. From the traditional English pubs like The Broadway Hotel, where a classic Sunday roast will cost around £18-£25, to elegant dining at places such as The Lygon Arms in nearby villages, the culinary scene caters to all tastes and budgets. For a more casual experience, several tea rooms offer homemade cakes and light lunches priced between £8-£15, ideal for a midday break.

Accommodation in Broadway suits a range of budgets. Charming bed and breakfasts can be found for £70-£100 per night in the off-season, while boutique hotels and country house inns typically start at £130 and can go up to £250 per night during peak times. Booking ahead, especially during spring and autumn festivals like the Broadway Arts Festival or the Christmas Market, is advisable.

Getting around Broadway is straightforward on foot, as the village is compact and walkable. For exploring the surrounding countryside, renting a bicycle is a great option, with local hire shops charging about £20-£30 per day. However, public buses are limited, so having a car will significantly enhance your ability to visit nearby attractions such as Snowshill Manor and Hidcote Gardens (both National Trust properties with entry fees around £10-£15).

Broadway's peaceful yet cultured vibe makes it perfect not only for day-trippers but also for longer stays where you want to unwind, explore countryside trails, and soak in the artistic heritage. It's a village that rewards the curious traveler with quiet moments on its village green, lively market days, and a wealth of local history and craftsmanship.

In summary, Broadway's combination of stunning architecture, excellent amenities, and prime location make it an essential stop in the Northern Cotswolds itinerary. It's a place to relax, explore, and enjoy a genuine slice of English village life without the rush or crowds found in larger towns.

Moreton-in-Marsh

Moreton-in-Marsh is a vibrant market town and a true gateway to the Northern Cotswolds, offering a perfect blend of historic charm, convenient transport links, and authentic local life. Situated in Gloucestershire, roughly 15 miles northeast of Cheltenham and about 90 miles northwest of London, Moreton-in-Marsh benefits from its strategic location on the edge of the Cotswolds Area of Outstanding Natural Beauty, making it an ideal base for exploring the region.

What makes Moreton-in-Marsh special is its status as both a bustling market town with a rich history and a practical hub for travelers. The town's origins date back to Roman times, and the main street retains much of its traditional character with honey-colored stone buildings and historic inns, like The Bell Inn, which dates back to the 15th century. Every Tuesday, the town hosts one of the largest traditional outdoor markets in the Cotswolds, offering everything from fresh local produce and antiques to crafts and clothing. This market is a highlight for visitors, providing a genuine slice of local life — entry is free, and it's best to arrive early to avoid the crowds.

For many visitors, Moreton-in-Marsh serves as a convenient entry point to the Cotswolds because of its excellent rail connections. The town is on the mainline railway between London Paddington and Worcester, with direct trains from London taking approximately 1 hour 20 minutes. Return fares booked in advance typically range from £20 to £40, making it an accessible day-trip destination or an ideal starting point for longer Cotswolds explorations. If driving, the town is easily reached via the A44, which connects to Oxford and Worcester, and there is ample parking available, typically costing £3-£6 per day.

Why visit Moreton-in-Marsh beyond the market? The town offers a gateway to many walking and cycling routes, including sections of the Cotswold Way National Trail. It's an excellent spot for outdoor enthusiasts looking to explore the rolling hills, ancient woodlands, and historic villages surrounding the area. For instance, a popular and manageable walk from the town leads to the ruins of Batsford Arboretum and Hidcote Manor Gardens, both roughly 3-5 miles away. Hidcote, a celebrated Arts and Crafts garden, charges around £13 for entry but is well worth it for garden lovers.

The town's accommodation options cater well to budget-conscious and mid-range travelers. There are a number of comfortable B&Bs and guesthouses offering rooms from about £60-£90 per night during low season, rising to around £120 on weekends or during events. Moreton also has several charming inns and boutique hotels such as The Redesdale Arms, which combines traditional English hospitality with modern comfort, with rooms from approximately £110 upwards. Booking ahead is advisable, especially during market days or local festivals like the annual Cotswold Games.

Eating out in Moreton-in-Marsh is a pleasure. You'll find a mix of traditional pubs and contemporary cafés, with prices ranging from hearty pub meals at £12-£20 to more upscale dining options offering tasting menus in the £30-£50 range. A standout is The Porch House, reputedly England's oldest inn, dating back to the 10th century, which serves excellent seasonal fare in a cozy historic setting.

Getting around Moreton-in-Marsh itself is straightforward, as the town is compact and walkable. However, for broader exploration, having a car is beneficial. There are limited bus services connecting to smaller villages in the area, but schedules can be infrequent and don't operate on Sundays, so plan accordingly. Taxis are available but can be costly for longer trips—expect to pay £20-£30 for journeys to nearby villages.

In essence, Moreton-in-Marsh is more than just a transit point; it's a lively town steeped in history with excellent facilities for visitors, making it an excellent base or stopover to experience authentic Cotswold life. Its combination of accessibility, cultural heritage, and local charm ensures that travelers leave with a strong impression of the Northern Cotswolds' unique character.

Snowshill: The Hidden Gem of the Cotswolds

Snowshill is one of those rare Cotswold villages that feels untouched by time — small, peaceful, and absolutely steeped in mystery and character. Located just 1.5 miles south of Broadway, in Gloucestershire, Snowshill sits at the edge of the northern escarpment of the Cotswold Hills, offering spectacular views across the Vale of Evesham. Despite being only a short drive from one of the region's most visited villages, it remains uncrowded and beautifully preserved — and that's part of its magic.

Why go?

Snowshill is known for two exceptional reasons: its breathtaking lavender fields and the eccentric and fascinating Snowshill Manor, both of which make it a destination worth going out of your way for.

Snowshill Lavender Farm, open from mid-June to early August, transforms the hillsides into sweeping seas of purple. I've personally visited multiple times, and every visit feels dreamlike. The scent, the silence, the colour — it's almost meditative. Entry is typically around £5–£7 per adult, and well worth it for photography, picnics, or simply sitting in peace. There's a lovely tearoom and a small gift shop selling handmade lavender goods. Tip: Go in early July when the lavender is at its peak but the school holiday crowds haven't arrived yet. If you're driving, there's free parking, but it's a 1.5-mile country lane from the village centre, so a car is essential.

Just a few minutes' walk from the village green, Snowshill Manor and Garden (a National Trust property) is an utterly unique experience. It's not your average stately home — it was the eccentric personal collection of Charles Wade, an artist and architect who spent his life amassing oddities and curiosities from around the world. The manor is full of Japanese samurai armour, musical instruments, tools, toys, masks, clocks, and more. Every room is a cabinet of wonders. Admission is around £14 for adults (free for National Trust members), and the surrounding terraced garden — designed to reflect Wade's theatrical flair — is a joy to explore. Allow at least 2 hours for a proper visit.

Getting there

Snowshill is best accessed by car. If you're coming from Broadway, it's a short 10-minute drive via Snowshill Road. From Moreton-in-Marsh, allow about 25 minutes (11 miles). There is no direct bus or train service to the village, which means it stays peaceful and free of coach tours — but also means public transport travelers will need a taxi or bike hire from nearby towns. Expect taxi fares from Broadway to cost around £12–£15 one-way. For those cycling from Broadway, be warned: it's a steep climb up the hill.

What it costs to visit

Snowshill is a great low-cost day trip for those already staying in the region. With a budget of £20–£30, you can easily cover a coffee and snack at the lavender farm, entrance to the manor, and maybe even a local souvenir. Parking in the village is limited, but free. Dining options are sparse — there's no pub in the village — but nearby Broadway (10 minutes away) offers plenty of options for lunch or dinner, from budget cafes to fine dining.

Why it's special

The quiet of Snowshill is profound. It's not commercialized — you won't find crowds or flashy shops here — and that's precisely why you go. The views are expansive. The golden stone cottages are wrapped in wisteria or roses depending on the season. You'll hear birdsong, maybe the distant murmur of a stream, and little else. At sunset, the light hits the hillside in a golden glow that photographers dream of capturing.

Snowshill isn't for those chasing nightlife or long itineraries. It's for those who want to slow down and really feel the Cotswolds — its beauty, its mystery, its stillness. Whether you're a photographer, garden lover, or simply need an escape from the over-touristed routes, this village delivers an experience that's rare and deeply personal.

Ebrington: The Quintessential Quiet Cotswold Village

Tucked away just 2 miles southeast of Chipping Campden, Ebrington is one of those places you almost don't want to tell people about because part of its magic lies in its serenity and under-the-radar charm. It's not a place you'll stumble across accidentally — you need to know it's there, and if you do, you'll be rewarded with an experience that feels genuinely local, authentic, and undisturbed.

Why go?

Ebrington offers a rare mix of unspoiled countryside beauty and superb food — and that's not something you often find in a village this size. The biggest draw here is The Ebrington Arms, a multi-award-winning thatched pub dating back to the 1640s. I've eaten there multiple times — the food is genuinely top-tier, using locally sourced ingredients, and the menu offers a modern British take on hearty classics. Expect mains to range from £17–£25, with a superb Sunday roast priced around £22. Their home-brewed ales (Yubby Ales) are well worth sampling, and the pub doubles as a cosy inn with rooms typically priced between £130–£170 per night depending on the season.

Walking around Ebrington is like stepping into a postcard — stone cottages draped in climbing roses, sheep-dotted meadows, and a church that dates to the 13th century. It's a popular starting point for countryside walks, including the 3-mile route to Hidcote Manor Gardens, which makes for an idyllic afternoon. Entry to Hidcote (National Trust) is £13, and it's one of the finest Arts and Crafts gardens in England — highly recommended in late spring and summer.

Getting There

Ebrington is best accessed by car, as there's no direct bus or train. From Chipping Campden, it's a 5-minute drive or a pleasant 40-minute walk through country paths. From Moreton-in-Marsh, it's about 25 minutes by car. If using public transport, your best bet is a train to Moreton-in-Marsh, then a taxi (approx. £20–£25 each way). The isolation is part of the appeal — you feel like you've truly escaped the modern world.

Cost-wise, aside from the cost of food or accommodation at the pub, visiting Ebrington can be a low-budget pleasure. Walking is free, the vibe is relaxed, and you won't find tourist traps or queues.

Verdict: Come to Ebrington if you crave quiet beauty, excellent food, and walks that soothe the soul. It's authentic, unfussy, and utterly charming — a real Cotswold treasure.

Blockley: The Cotswolds' Gol with Italian Vibes

At first glance, Blockley lool Cotswold villages — beautiful stone buildings, peaceful lanes, and flower-filled gardens. But once you explore it a little deeper, you'll notice it has a completely different energy. Tucked between Moreton-in-Marsh and Broadway, this hillside village is full of personality, with a long silk mill history and an almost Mediterranean feel — something I noticed instantly during my first visit in early summer. The ochre stone glows gold in the sun, and the steep, narrow streets almost resemble an Italian hill town.

Why go?

Blockley is a place for travelers who want to slow down and blend in. It's less polished and curated than places like Bourton-on-the-Water or Stow, and that's exactly why I keep returning. It has real life in it — a lived-in beauty that balances charm with character.

The Church of St. Peter and St. Paul is perhaps the village's most iconic landmark, especially since it gained recognition as the filming location for the "Father Brown" TV series. If you're a fan, you'll recognize much of the village instantly — but even if not, the church is lovely to visit and often open to the public.

There's a community-run café and shop that's a local institution: Blockley Village Shop & Café. It's a great place for a proper coffee, lunch (quiches, soups, and salads around £7–£10), or stocking up on local cheeses and Cotswold goodies. There's also a small botanical garden (Mill Dene Garden), open seasonally (£7 entry), that's surprisingly lush and creative — tucked into the side of a steep hill with ponds, terraces, and a working water mill.

Getting There

Blockley is just 3 miles from Moreton-in-Marsh. If you're driving, it takes about 8 minutes via the B4479. Public transport options are very limited, so your best bet is to take a train to Moreton and then a taxi (£10–£15) or a pre-booked bicycle rental if you're feeling energetic — just be ready for hills. Parking in the village is free but limited.

Accommodation in Blockley is a mix of self-catering cottages and a few boutique B&Bs. I've stayed in a charming Airbnb cottage that cost about £90 per night in shoulder season (April/October). Prices rise in summer, so book early. You won't find large hotels here, but that's what keeps the atmosphere peaceful and genuine.

What makes it special?

Blockley's combination of history, artistry, and authentic community makes it one of my top hidden gems in the Cotswolds. There's an old-world creativity about the place — from stone walls covered in clematis to the quirky carved benches dotted around the village. It's a destination for those who enjoy wandering without an agenda, discovering village lanes, chatting with locals in the café, and feeling like they've stumbled onto something special.

Central Cotswold Highlights

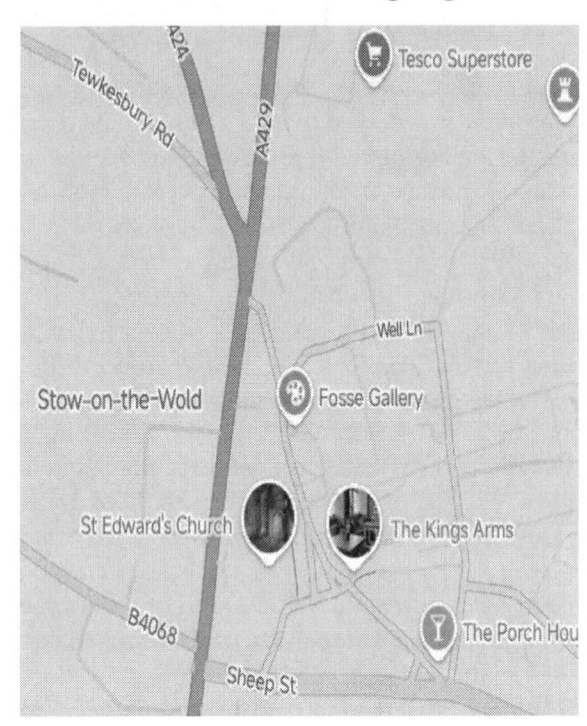

Stow-on-the-Wold: Market Town Majesty with Ancient Roots and Lively Spirit

Perched high on a hill at nearly 800 feet, Stow-on-the-Wold is not just one of the most iconic Cotswold towns — it's one of the most atmospheric and enduring. I've visited Stow repeatedly over the years and can honestly say it offers a perfect balance: steeped in medieval history, buzzing with antique shops and independent boutiques, but still authentic and unpretentious. This town is not just a postcard setting — it's a lived-in place where real stories, real people, and rich traditions converge.

Why Go?

Stow's charm lies in its combination of historic importance, central location, and vibrant market-town energy. It was a major wool trading hub in medieval England, and you can still feel that legacy in the town's wide market square, which was once used to herd sheep in by the thousands. The square remains the heart of the

40

town — surrounded by honey-coloured townhouses, antique shops, bookstores, and some of the best tearooms and pubs in the region.

It's also home to one of the most photographed doors in the Cotswolds — the Norman north door of St. Edward's Church, famously flanked by ancient yew trees and rumored (probably inaccurately) to have inspired Tolkien's Doors of Durin. Even so, it's a magical spot.

For shoppers, Stow is an antique hunter's dream. Try Tara Antiques or The Curiosity Shop, where I've found everything from Edwardian maps to 19th-century apothecary bottles. Prices vary wildly — some finds are under £30, while rarer items go for hundreds.

What to Do

- **St. Edward's Church (free to enter):** A peaceful medieval church dating back to the 11th century. Step inside for a quiet moment and admire the stained glass and carved wood.
- **Shopping:** Antiques, artisan food, tweeds, and books abound. Check out Borzoi Bookshop — one of the region's best independent bookstores.
- **Dining:** You're spoiled for choice. I recommend:
    - **The Porch House** – England's oldest inn, dating to 947 AD. Great for hearty fare and ales. Mains £16–£26.
    - **Cotswold Baguettes** – ideal for takeaways or picnic supplies (sandwiches around £5–£7).
    - **Lucy's Tearoom** – classic Cotswold afternoon tea spot (cream tea for £8.95).

If you visit on a Thursday, the farmers' market in the square is worth your time — local cheeses, breads, crafts, and handmade gifts.

Getting There

Stow-on-the-Wold is centrally located, making it a convenient base or stopover. It lies at the junction of the Fosse Way (A429) and the A436.

- **By Train:** There's no train station in Stow itself. The nearest is Moreton-in-Marsh (5 miles away), which has direct trains from London Paddington (approx. 1 hr 30 min, £25–£45 one-way depending on time and class). From there, it's a 10-minute taxi ride (£12–£15) or a bus (Pulhams 801, approx. £3.50).
- **By Car:** From Oxford, it's around 50 minutes (via A44). From Cheltenham, about 30 minutes. Parking in town is surprisingly decent — the free long-stay car park on Maugersbury Road is your best bet.

Where to Stay

Stow offers a strong mix of accommodation, with prices reflecting its popularity — slightly higher than smaller villages, especially in peak season (May–September).

- **Budget:** The Bell at Stow – rooms from around £100 per night in low season.
- **Mid-range:** The Kings Arms – charming coaching inn with character; expect to pay £130–£180 per night.
- **Luxury:** The Porch House – for a historical experience and luxury finish, expect £180–£250 per night.

Airbnb also has several options — you can find well-rated cottages or annex flats starting from £85/night in shoulder seasons.

Cost Overview

For a typical visit:

- **Accommodation:** £100–£180/night (depending on season and type)
- **Meals:** £25–£50/day for casual dining; more for fine dining
- **Transport:** Train + taxi from London around £40–£60 one-way total
- **Shopping & experiences:** Flexible, but even browsing antiques is half the fun

Final Thoughts

Stow-on-the-Wold is a place where the past and present truly coexist. Whether you're sipping ale in a 1,000-year-old inn, chatting with a local cheese-maker at the market, or wandering side streets with a fresh pastry in hand, the town rewards those who slow down. It's central, well-connected, and full of character — a must-visit if you're exploring the Cotswolds properly.

Bourton-on-the-Water: The "Venice of the Cotswolds" — With More Charm and Fewer Gondolas

Bourton-on-the-Water is one of the most beloved villages in the Cotswolds, and it's easy to see why. Nestled along the gentle River Windrush, the village is famed for its low stone bridges, golden limestone buildings, and willow-shaded greens. It's consistently voted one of the prettiest villages in England — and while it can get busy, it's popular for good reason.

I've visited Bourton in every season — from sunny summer afternoons when the village buzzes with families enjoying ice cream by the river, to crisp December mornings when fairy lights twinkle above the stone bridges. No matter when you go, the village offers a rare combination of natural beauty, walkability, attractions, and accessible dining and accommodation — making it perfect for both day trips and overnight stays.

Why Go?

Unlike some Cotswold villages that offer only a quiet stroll and a photo op, Bourton is activity-packed without feeling over-commercialized. It's an ideal base for first-time visitors who want a village that's easy to explore but full of options. There's something whimsical about sitting beside the River Windrush with a cream tea, watching ducks float under 18th-century bridges — and then being able to walk to a model village, perfume factory, or wildlife park, all within a 10-minute radius.

The town centre is compact, flat, and very walkable. The stone bridges crossing the Windrush are picture-perfect, and the village green is one of the loveliest picnic spots in the Cotswolds.

Top Things to Do

- **The Model Village (entry £5.50 adults, £4.50 children):** A Grade II-listed 1:9 scale replica of Bourton itself, built in the 1930s from local stone. Surprisingly intricate and a joy to explore.
- **Cotswold Motoring Museum (entry £7.50 adults, £5.25 children):** An absolute treat if you're into vintage cars, motorcycles, or British nostalgia. Even if you're not a petrolhead, the memorabilia is fascinating.
- **Birdland Park & Gardens (entry £12.95 adults, £8.95 children):** A family-friendly wildlife park home to penguins, flamingos, owls, and parrots.

- Great for children, and the penguin feeding is oddly therapeutic.
- **Greystones Nature Reserve (free):** Just a 5-minute walk from the village centre, this peaceful reserve has wildflower meadows, Iron Age ruins, and beautiful walking trails.
- **Dragonfly Maze (£5 adults, £4 children):** A quirky hedge maze with a twist — you solve clues as you go to reach the centre. Simple but fun.

Food & Drink

- **Bakery on the Water:** My personal favorite for a morning pastry or light lunch. Their sourdough and almond croissants are worth queueing for (pastries £3–£4.50, sandwiches around £7).
- **The Rose Tree:** A riverside restaurant that's excellent for traditional British dishes done well. Expect mains around £16–£24.
- **The Croft:** Lovely setting, perfect for brunch or a warm scone by the river (£8–£12).
- **Smiths of Bourton:** A stylish burger joint that breaks from the typical country fare. Burgers start around £13, and the truffle fries are fantastic.

Cream teas in most cafés will cost about £8.50–£10 per person. You'll find options for all budgets, but expect slightly higher prices in peak season.

Getting There

Bourton-on-the-Water is located in Gloucestershire, just off the A429, and well connected to other key towns like Stow-on-the-Wold and Moreton-in-Marsh.

- **By Train:** There is no direct station in Bourton. The closest station is Moreton-in-Marsh (9 miles), which is on the direct line from London Paddington (journey time approx. 1 hr 35 min, tickets £25–£45). From there, take a local taxi (around £20–£25) or Pulhams bus 801 (approx. £3.50 one-way).
- **By Car:** Bourton is easily reached from Oxford (1 hour via A40), Cheltenham (30 minutes), and London (2 hours). Public parking is available at Rissington Road Car Park (GL54 2BN) — £4–£6 for the day.

Where to Stay

Accommodations here range from historic inns to stylish B&Bs and riverside cottages. Prices spike during holidays and summer weekends, so early booking is essential.

- **The Dial House Hotel** – Elegant Georgian manor with well-appointed rooms and excellent service. Rooms from £160–£250 per night.
- **Chester House Hotel** – A mid-range favorite in the centre of the village. Rates around £125–£180/night with breakfast.
- **The Lansdowne** – Classic B&B with great hosts and comfortable rooms. Doubles from £100–£150.
- Airbnb options include riverside flats and quaint stone cottages, starting from around £85–£130 per night in low or shoulder season.

Cost Overview for a Day Visit (Per Person)

- **Transport:** Train + bus/taxi from London approx. £35–£50 return

- **Attractions:** £15–£25 depending on how many you visit
- **Food:** £20–£40 depending on dining choices
- **Souvenirs or local products:** Optional, but plan £10–£30

Total day trip estimate: £70–£120, depending on choices

Final Word

Bourton-on-the-Water isn't just charming — it's one of the best-rounded villages in the Cotswolds. Whether you're planning a romantic couple's weekend, a solo photography trip, or a family day out, it delivers scenery, substance, and a strong sense of place. Yes, it can get busy in peak season — but even then, it manages to retain its magic.

If you're mapping out a multi-stop Cotswolds itinerary, Bourton is an essential stop — or better yet, spend the night and enjoy the village when the day-trippers leave and the light glows golden on the honey-stone bridges.

Lower Slaughter & Upper Slaughter: Cotswolds Serenity at Its Finest

If you're looking for a slice of the Cotswolds that still feels untouched, where time seems to pause and the only sound might be the trickle of a stream or birdsong over a stone bridge — then Lower and Upper Slaughter are essential stops. These twin villages, located just a mile apart, are two of the most beautifully preserved and quietly elegant places in all of England. I've returned here again and again — each time craving their rare sense of calm and authenticity.

While Bourton-on-the-Water (just 1.5 miles away) buzzes with visitors and activity, the Slaughters offer a more secluded and romantic charm, with far fewer crowds and a stunning riverside setting. They're perfect for slow, mindful travel, countryside photography, and peaceful exploration — and for me, they feel like the soul of the Cotswolds.

Why Visit?

The Slaughters are quintessentially Cotswold, but without the commercial gloss. You won't find souvenir shops or long café queues here — instead, you'll walk along the River Eye, past stone cottages that haven't changed in centuries, through meadows, and into history. The name "Slaughter" might be off-putting, but it actually comes from the Old English slothre, meaning "muddy place" — though in truth, these villages are anything but.

They are especially great for:

- Romantic getaways
- Scenic walking holidays
- Historic charm lovers
- Photographers and painters
- Those wanting a break from crowds

Lower Slaughter

Lower Slaughter is the more visited of the two, and for good reason. The village is built along the River Eye, with charming stone footbridges, willow trees dipping into the water, and well-tended gardens that bloom vibrantly in spring and summer.

The highlight is the Old Mill Museum, a 19th-century watermill (entry approx. £4.50) complete with a working mill wheel, a café, and a small shop selling handmade crafts and local fudge. The riverside path near the mill is one of the most peaceful walks in the Cotswolds — ideal for a picnic or reflective moment.

If you're up for a treat, The Slaughters Country Inn offers exceptional food in a relaxed setting — think Cotswold chicken, seasonal veg, and beautifully plated desserts. Lunch mains run around £17–£24, with a set two-course option sometimes available at lunchtime for £25–£28. It's also a wonderful spot to stay (rooms from £130–£200/night, depending on the season).

Upper Slaughter

Upper Slaughter is often even quieter than its sister — it's one of the rare "Doubly Thankful Villages", meaning it lost no soldiers in both World Wars. That history contributes to the peaceful aura that lingers here. The village is built around a gentle hill, and while it's tiny (you can walk through it in 10 minutes), it's incredibly photogenic and serene.

There's no commercial centre, no shops — just perfect architecture, a 12th-century church (St. Peter's), and winding lanes. A circular walk from Lower to Upper Slaughter and back takes around 45 minutes at a gentle pace, with scenic countryside paths in between. It's one of the best short hikes in the region.

For a luxurious experience, Lords of the Manor Hotel, a converted rectory turned country house hotel, is located here. It's quiet, refined, and ideal for those wanting a more exclusive retreat. Dinner here is a fine-dining experience, with multi-course tasting menus starting at £70–£95 per person, and rooms starting from £230 per night.

Getting There

Location: Both villages are located in Gloucestershire, in the heart of the North Cotswolds. They lie just 1.5 miles west of Bourton-on-the-Water and 3 miles south of Stow-on-the-Wold.

- **By Car:** The easiest and most practical way to get to the Slaughters. From London, it's about a 2-hour drive (via M40 and A429). From Oxford, it takes just over an hour.
- **By Train:** The nearest station is Moreton-in-Marsh, with trains from London Paddington (journey time approx. 1 hr 40 mins, tickets £25–£45). From there, a taxi to Lower Slaughter takes 15–20 minutes and costs around £25–£30.
- **By Bus:** There is limited bus service (Pulhams 801 to Bourton), but not directly to the Slaughters. Best to arrive in Bourton and walk or take a taxi from there.

Walking Route Suggestion

One of the most rewarding ways to experience the Slaughters is on foot:

- Start in Bourton-on-the-Water
- Walk to Lower Slaughter (25 minutes, flat and scenic)
- Then continue to Upper Slaughter (another 20 minutes through countryside paths)
- Return the same way or loopback via a different route through meadows

This short 4-mile round-trip is one of the most peaceful half-day experiences in the Cotswolds.

Best Time to Visit

Late spring through early autumn (May–September) is ideal for warm weather and blooming gardens. Autumn (late September to October) brings stunning golden foliage, and even winter has its charm — especially with a light dusting of snow. The villages are stunning at golden hour, so if you can stay overnight and catch a sunrise or sunset, it's magical.

Final Word

The Slaughters offer a slower, more soulful Cotswolds experience. They're not for thrill-seekers or shopaholics, but for those who appreciate beauty in simplicity, quiet in nature, and deep historical roots. For romantics, writers, photographers, and anyone needing a pause from modern life — this is where you go to reconnect with something timeless.

Even after visiting dozens of villages across the Cotswolds, I always return to the Slaughters. They don't shout for attention — and that's precisely what makes them unforgettable.

Kingham: A Refined Village with Rural Elegance

Kingham is one of those rare Cotswold villages that offers a perfect balance between quiet country charm and sophisticated rural living. Nestled in the Evenlode Valley in Oxfordshire, just 4 miles southwest of Chipping Norton and 6 miles from Stow-on-the-Wold, Kingham feels like a well-kept secret — yet it has quietly become a favourite escape for Londoners and slow travellers alike. It's been named one of England's most beautiful villages multiple times, and after several visits, I completely understand why.

The honey-hued stone cottages, immaculately kept village green, and peaceful atmosphere are classic Cotswolds. But what really sets Kingham apart is its accessibility and culinary scene.

Why Go?

- Scenic walking routes and idyllic countryside
- A direct rail link to London — one of the few truly rural villages in the Cotswolds with its own train station
- Top-tier dining at The Wild Rabbit and The Kingham Plough
- A great base for exploring nearby Bourton, Stow, and Daylesford

Kingham's rail station is a major asset. You can reach it directly from London Paddington in about 1 hour 25 minutes, and a return ticket generally costs £40–£60 depending on time of booking. From the station, it's a 15-minute walk into the village.

Where to Eat

The Wild Rabbit is a beautifully renovated 18th-century inn with organic, seasonal menus and minimalist-chic interiors. It's one of the best gastropubs in England — expect mains from £28–£40, with a lunch menu sometimes available at £35 for two courses. I've had incredible venison here, and their wine list is superb.

The Kingham Plough, just across the green, offers a more rustic and casual experience, but the food is consistently good (mains from £20–£30), and the service is warm without being fussy.

Where to Stay

You can stay at either of the above inns, with rooms ranging from £150–£300 per night, or opt for self-catering cottages via Airbnb or local rental sites. Expect a decent self-catering cottage to start around £120–£160/night, especially off-season.

Walks & Nature

From Kingham, there are several circular walks through rolling farmland and quiet woods. One of my favourites is the Kingham to Churchill loop — about 5 miles — which takes you past stone walls, grazing sheep, and timeless countryside vistas.

Naunton: Off-the-Beaten-Path Beauty with a Historic Core

Tucked in a valley along the River Windrush, Naunton is one of the most authentic and overlooked villages in the central Cotswolds. Located about 5 miles east of Bourton-on-the-Water, it's quiet, picturesque, and largely untouched by mass tourism.

What makes Naunton stand out is its watermill, cricket ground, and the beautifully preserved St. Andrew's Church, which dates back to the 13th century. The heart of the village is a winding street of honey-coloured cottages that feels straight out of a historical film set — and yet, it's lived in and loved, not overly polished.

There are no tourist shops, no big coach tours, and that's the appeal. It's a village for walkers, photographers, and those wanting to see what the Cotswolds were like before the crowds.

Getting There

Naunton is best accessed by car — it's about a 10-minute drive from Bourton or 20 minutes from Stow-on-the-Wold. If you're staying in those hubs, consider making this a half-day detour or walking destination. There are limited buses, and taxis from Bourton cost around £15–£20 one way.

Walking Tip

The Naunton to Guiting Power trail is an 8km walk (roughly 5 miles) through idyllic landscapes, passing quiet farms and open hills. Bring good boots — it can be muddy in spring and autumn — but it's absolutely worth it.

Bledington: A Tranquil Cotswold Treasure

Just 2 miles from Kingham sits Bledington, a peaceful and charming village known for its village green, duck pond, and The King's Head Inn — a local pub with award-winning food and very comfortable rooms.

Bledington is smaller and even quieter than Kingham, but what I love about it is the unhurried pace and community feel. On summer evenings, locals gather around the green, children play near the stream, and there's often a faint sound of clinking pint glasses from the inn. It's what I'd call an "authentic slow England" experience.

Why Go?

- For peace and privacy
- A perfect base if Kingham is booked out or overpriced
- Excellent walking access — especially the Oxfordshire Way trail

Where to Stay & Eat

The King's Head Inn is the centre of village life here, offering high-end pub fare (mains from £22–£30) and well-appointed rooms (£130–£200/night, including breakfast). I stayed here one autumn weekend — the rooms were warm and characterful, and the sticky toffee pudding was unforgettable.

Getting There

Like Naunton, Bledington is best accessed by car or from Kingham Station, which is just a 20–25 minute walk or a £10–£12 taxi ride. You can also walk between Kingham and Bledington easily via public footpaths through meadows — it's a lovely 1.5-mile stroll that only takes about 30–40 minutes.

Final Thoughts

If you want to truly slow down and appreciate the soul of the Cotswolds — away from the more heavily promoted stops — then Kingham, Naunton, and Bledington are the places to be. They don't shout for your attention but reward you with timeless architecture, culinary excellence, peaceful walking routes, and a sense that you've stepped into an older, quieter England.

I always recommend these three villages to travelers who want to go beyond the checklist and actually experience the rhythm of local life. They're perfect for writers, walkers, foodies, and anyone seeking the kind of authenticity that's becoming rarer each year in the Cotswolds.

Southern Cotswolds Highlights: Cirencester — The Capital of the Cotswolds

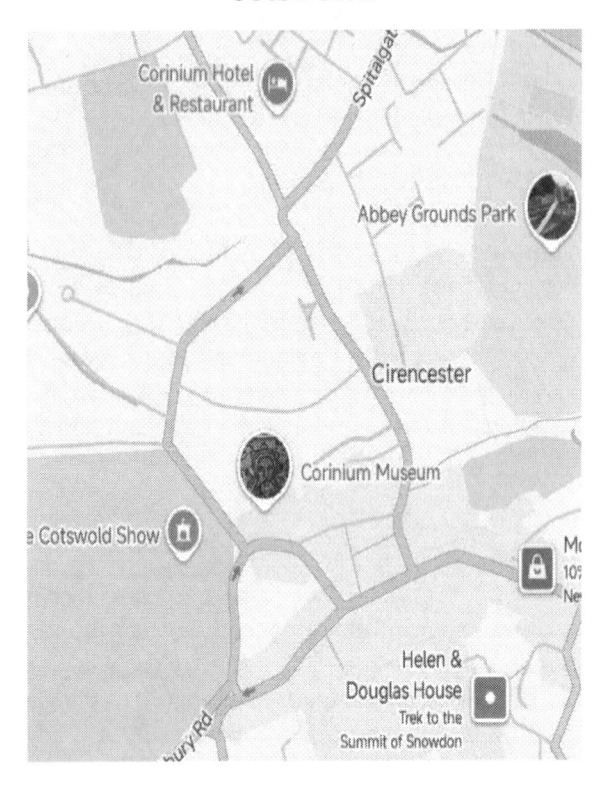

Often called the "Capital of the Cotswolds," Cirencester is a must-visit for travelers wanting to delve deeper into the historical, cultural, and everyday life of the region. It's the largest market town in the Cotswolds, located in Gloucestershire, and has a vibrant energy that smaller villages may lack — without sacrificing the honey-stone charm and relaxed pace the Cotswolds are known for.

Just under 100 miles west of London, Cirencester is easily accessible yet remains blissfully untouched by the overly touristy feel of places like Bourton-on-the-Water. I've visited Cirencester multiple times, and each time, the fusion of Roman history, artisan markets, leafy parks, and excellent cafés has offered a deeper appreciation of the region.

Why Visit Cirencester?

There are three main reasons to make Cirencester a central stop on your Southern Cotswolds route:

1. **Roman History:** Cirencester was once Corinium Dobunnorum, the second-largest town in Roman Britain. Today, you can see well-preserved relics at the Corinium Museum — a highlight of any cultural itinerary.

2. **Markets & Shopping:** Cirencester's thriving market culture, boutique shops, and indie eateries offer a slice of daily life that feels both timeless and current.

3. **Great Base for Exploration:** With its range of accommodations and solid transport links, Cirencester makes an ideal base for exploring Tetbury, Bibury, Cricklade, and Westonbirt Arboretum.

How to Get There

- **From London by Train:** Take a train from London Paddington to Kemble Station (about 1 hour 15 minutes, with tickets costing between £30–£50 return depending on booking time). From Kemble, it's a 10-minute taxi ride to Cirencester (£10–£15), or you can take the limited local bus (Stagecoach 882).

- **By Car:** Cirencester sits just off the A417/A429 junction. Driving from London takes around 2–2.5 hours depending on traffic. It's well-connected from Oxford, Bath, and Cheltenham.

- **Parking:** Ample paid parking is available throughout the town. The Beeches Car Park and Forum Car Park are central and affordable, usually around £2 for 2 hours, £4.50 all-day.

Top Things to Do in Cirencester

- **Corinium Museum:** This is the best Roman museum in the region, housing mosaics, coins, and artifacts from Cirencester's ancient past. Entry is £7.40 adults, £3.70 children, and worth every penny if you enjoy history.

- **Cirencester Park:** Owned by the Bathurst family, this stunning parkland is free to enter and perfect for a morning walk or afternoon picnic. The formal park gives way to wild, tree-lined avenues stretching for miles — a real treat in spring and autumn.

- **Parish Church of St. John the Baptist:** One of the largest parish churches in England, this towering landmark dominates the town square. It's free to enter, and guided tours are sometimes available.

- **Market Days: The** Charter Market takes place on Mondays and Fridays, offering everything from local produce to antiques and handmade crafts. It's ideal for grabbing a snack or buying genuine souvenirs like Cotswold-made ceramics or handmade soaps.

Where to Eat

Cirencester has a food scene that's far more evolved than most towns its size in the Cotswolds.

- **Jesse's Bistro (on Black Jack Street) is a gem for lunch** — offering seasonal British plates like Cotswold lamb or smoked trout salad. Mains average around £16–£22.

- Made by Bob, located in the Corn Hall Arcade, is a stylish deli-bistro hybrid. Expect artisan cheeses, fresh baked breads, and well-crafted mains from around £14–£25. Great coffee too.

- For budget travelers, The Fleece (a local pub) offers hearty meals with mains from £13–£18, and a charming, wood-beamed interior.

Where to Stay

Cirencester has accommodation options for every budget:

- The Kings Head Hotel (4-star, central) blends boutique design with original features. Rooms from £120–£200/night, depending on season.

- The Fleece at Cirencester is a cozy, historic inn with rooms above the pub — expect £100–£160/night, with breakfast included.

- Budget travelers might opt for Airbnbs or self-catering cottages in the area — you can find 1-bedroom cottages from £80–£110/night, especially if booking midweek or in off-peak months (Jan–Mar, Nov).

Nearby Day Trips from Cirencester

- **Bibury:** A 15-minute drive away. Visit Arlington Row and the trout farm. Beautiful in the early morning or at dusk to avoid the crowds.
- **Tetbury:** 20 minutes by car. Home to antique shops, Prince Charles's Highgrove shop, and Westonbirt Arboretum (entry £13–£15).
- **Chedworth Roman Villa:** About 25 minutes' drive — one of Britain's most impressive Roman villas, with floor

till in situ. Entry £11.50 adults, Trust members free.

Cirencester is not just a pretty Cotswold town — it's a living, breathing market hub with deep historical roots and modern sophistication. Whether you're a history enthusiast, nature lover, or simply want a more grounded Cotswolds base that's still beautiful and atmospheric, Cirencester offers a rich experience without the tour bus queues.

It's also a practical choice: great food, excellent walking access, stylish but affordable stays, and useful transport connections. For anyone spending more than a day or two in the Southern Cotswolds, Cirencester deserves a firm place on your itinerary.

Tetbury – Regal Charm and Antique Treasures in the Southern Cotswolds

Tetbury is a refined, elegant market town tucked into the southern Cotswolds, just a 20-minute drive from Cirencester and about 30 minutes from Bath. This isn't just any sleepy village — it's a town with strong royal connections and an unmistakable sense of quiet affluence. Tetbury is best known as the home of Highgrove House, the private residence of King Charles III, and it wears this distinction with pride.

What sets Tetbury apart is its regal atmosphere, upmarket independent shops, and antique hunting culture. If you're the kind of traveler who appreciates beautifully preserved Georgian architecture, loves browsing antique shops, and enjoys a town with a slower, elegant pace — Tetbury should absolutely be on your itinerary.

Getting There:

- **By Car:** Easily accessible via the A433, Tetbury is roughly 45 minutes from Bristol, and 30 minutes from the M4 motorway at junction 17.
- **By Train:** The nearest station is Kemble, about 20 minutes away by taxi. A direct train from London Paddington to Kemble takes 75–90 minutes and costs around £30–£50 return.
- **Parking:** Ample parking is available at West Street car park and The Chipping, both centrally located and about £2 for 2 hours or £5 per day.

Things to Do:

- **Visit Highgrove Gardens (Seasonal):** Open from April to October, the guided garden tours are a delight for horticulture lovers. Tickets cost around £30–£35 per adult and include access to the gardens and tea rooms. Booking well in advance is essential.
- **Antique Shopping:** Tetbury has more than 20 antique shops, many housed in historic stone buildings. Prices vary widely — you can pick up a collectible item for £30, or spend thousands on restored furnishings.
- **Tetbury Market House:** The iconic pillared Market House, dating from the 1600s, is in the town center and often hosts craft fairs and art shows. Entry is usually free.
- **Parish Church of St Mary the Virgin:** With one of the tallest spires in the Cotswolds, this beautiful church is worth a peaceful visit — especially around golden hour.

Where to Eat:

- The Close Hotel offers stylish British dining in a sophisticated setting. Mains start at around £20–£30.
- For budget-conscious travelers, Lettie's Bistro and Casa La Cucina Italiana both offer filling meals from £10–£18.

- Don't miss **The Priory Inn** for wood-fired pizzas and a great Cotswold ale selection — excellent value and a relaxed setting.

Where to Stay:

- The Close Hotel and The Priory Inn offer boutique rooms from £110–£180/night.
- Budget travelers should check Airbnb or The Snooty Fox, where rates begin at £90/night, especially in shoulder seasons (March/November).

Nailsworth – Artistic Soul of the South Cotswolds

Just 4 miles from Tetbury, the town of Nailsworth feels like a well-kept secret, especially for travelers looking for charm without the coach loads. It's a place where creative spirit, eco-conscious living, and laid-back Cotswold style intersect. Nailsworth is smaller and quieter than Tetbury, but full of personality — a town with working water mills, artisan bakeries, and a reputation for excellent food.

I've always found Nailsworth to be refreshingly unpretentious, with a genuinely local vibe. It's ideal if you're into browsing art galleries, walking along canal paths, or tucking into top-quality, locally sourced meals.

Getting There:

- **By Car:** Just a 10-minute drive from Tetbury or 25 minutes from Stroud, via the B4014.
- **By Train:** The closest station is Stroud, with frequent trains from London Paddington (1hr 30min, £30–£50 return). From Stroud, you can take a 10-minute taxi (£12–£15) or a Stagecoach local bus (approx. £3.50).

Things to Do:

- **Explore Artisan Shops:** Nailsworth is known for its boutique shops. Don't miss Domestic Science (homewares and crafts), The Yellow-Lighted Bookshop, and Raffles Fine Wines.
- **Ruskin Mill and Horsley Valley Walks:** You can take a tranquil walk through the valley past trout ponds and woods. Completely free and incredibly peaceful — it feels like stepping into a lost world.
- **Cycling & Canal Paths:** The Stroudwater Canal restoration has made Nailsworth a good base for walking or cycling day trips toward Stroud and beyond.

Where to Eat:

- **The Wild Garlic (Michelin-recommended):** A small bistro offering locally-sourced, seasonal cuisine. Mains around £22–£30 — worth the splurge.

- For lighter bites or brunch, head to The Canteen or Hobbs House Bakery — both excellent, with meals and pastries from £6–£12.

Where to Stay:

- The Egypt Mill Hotel is set in a restored mill with characterful rooms. Expect to pay £95–£150/night, with breakfast included.

- Airbnb options are plentiful and cozy — a room or cottage ranges from £70–£100/night, depending on season.

Why Go to Tetbury and Nailsworth?

Both towns offer a richer, more grounded Cotswolds experience, especially for return travelers or those looking to go beyond the postcard villages. Tetbury offers elegance, history, and shopping; Nailsworth delivers creativity, food culture, and nature walks. They're close enough to each other to pair in one base (you can easily stay in one and day-trip to the other), yet different enough to offer contrasting experiences.

If you're traveling without a car, Tetbury is a stronger base due to better taxi access from Kemble. With a car, staying in Nailsworth gives you more relaxed charm and easier access to off-the-beaten-track nature walks.

Painswick – The Queen of the Cotswolds

Nicknamed "The Queen of the Cotswolds," Painswick is a remarkably well-preserved wool town nestled in the Gloucestershire hills, about 10 minutes from Stroud and 20 minutes from Gloucester. What makes Painswick truly special is its timeless architecture, steep narrow lanes, and breathtaking hilltop views over the Slad Valley — made famous by writer Laurie Lee in Cider with Rosie.

Painswick isn't as busy as Broadway or Bourton, and that's its strength. You come here to slow down, to walk through centuries-old churchyards, and to explore hidden gardens and artsy corners in peace. It's one of the most atmospheric places I've stayed — there's an almost spiritual calm that settles over the town, especially in early morning or dusk.

Getting There:

- **By Car:** Just 3 miles from Stroud via the B4070. From London, it's about 2.5 hours by car.
- **By Train:** Take a direct train from London Paddington to Stroud (about 1h 30m, £30–£50 return), then a taxi to Painswick (10 minutes, approx. £12–£15).
- **Bus:** The Stagecoach 66 bus runs between Cheltenham and Stroud, stopping in Painswick.

Top Things to Do:

- **St Mary's Churchyard:** Famed for its 99 ancient yew trees, the church and its grounds are hauntingly beautiful and completely free to explore.

- **Painswick Rococo Garden:** The only surviving 18th-century rococo garden in England. It's a magical escape, particularly in early spring when the snowdrops bloom. Entry is £9.50 for adults, and it's worth every penny.

- **Slad Valley Walks:** Painswick is a gateway to some of the best walks in the Cotswolds. Try the Laurie Lee Wildlife Way, a 5-mile circular route dotted with poetry posts. Totally free and endlessly scenic.

Where to Eat & Stay:

- The Painswick Hotel offers top-tier dining and boutique accommodation. Rooms start from £150–£200 per night, and it's worth it for the view and service.

- Falcon Inn is a great alternative — more traditional, with rooms starting around £110–£130.

- For dining, try The Oak for hearty local fare (mains £15–£22) or St Michael's Bistro for European dishes and a lovely courtyard garden.

Minchinhampton – Hilltop Beauty & Common Land Walks

A true hidden gem, Minchinhampton sits on a hill overlooking the Stroud valleys, surrounded by the vast open space of Minchinhampton Common — over 500 acres of protected common land where cows roam freely from spring to autumn. This is the kind of place where you walk out of your charming stone cottage straight onto miles of scenic trails.

What I love about Minchinhampton is its unpolished authenticity. It's not overly touristy, but it's rich in character. The narrow high street has a local bakery, a proper butcher, and a tiny Market House from the 1600s. It's one of those Cotswold villages that feels lived in and loved.

Getting There:

- **By Car:** About 10 minutes from Stroud or Nailsworth. Roads are steep and winding, but views are stunning.
- **Public Transport:** Stroud is the nearest train station. From there, take a taxi (approx. £10–£12). Buses are limited.

What to Do:

- **Minchinhampton Common Walks:** Ideal for a picnic or a breezy stroll. It's common land managed by the National Trust and free to access. Sunset here is spectacular.
- The Kitchen in the Market Square is a hidden foodie haven — fantastic brunches and homemade cakes (meals from £8–£14).
- **Amberley Inn (nearby):** Great for a pint or a quiet overnight stay near the edge of the common (rooms from £120).

Cost Tip:

Parking on the Common is free. There are no entrance fees for the walks, so it's ideal for budget-conscious travelers.

Bisley – A Hidden Time Capsule with Rich Traditions

If you want to truly step back in time, head to Bisley, a secluded and utterly peaceful village northeast of Stroud. Bisley is smaller than Painswick or Minchinhampton but no less beautiful — cobbled paths, medieval cottages, and ancient wells still dressed every May in an old tradition that dates back centuries.

This village is steeped in Cotswold tradition and has avoided the mainstream tourism radar, which makes it a rare find. Even as someone who's spent years exploring the region, Bisley still feels like a secret. It's best for those looking to disconnect, walk, write, or soak up rural England without distraction.

Getting There:

- **By Car:** About 15 minutes from Stroud via narrow country roads. GPS is a must.
- **By Train & Taxi:** Train to Stroud, then taxi to Bisley (£15–£18, as it's a bit more remote).

Things to Do:

- **The Wells & May Well Dressing:** Visit in early May if you can — the flower-dressed wells are a local treasure, and the whole village joins in.
- **Walks Around the Toadsmoor Valley:** Woodland, meadows, and big sky views. Pack walking boots — it gets muddy.
- **St. Mary's Church:** Tranquil, atmospheric, and with a churchyard that feels like something from a gothic novel.

Where to Stay & Eat:

- The Bear Inn offers a cozy pub atmosphere with occasional live music and Cotswold ales. Great for a meal under £20.

- Cottage stays and self-catering Airbnb options start around £85–£110 per night, perfect for couples or walkers.

Final Thoughts: Why These Villages Matter

If you want to move beyond the postcard crowds and experience the soul of the Southern Cotswolds, Painswick, Minchinhampton, and

Bisley deliver in spades. Each offers something unique:

- Painswick is architectural and cultural.
- Minchinhampton is windswept and wide open.
- Bisley is tucked away and utterly timeless.

They're perfect for travelers seeking depth, quiet beauty, and authenticity. You'll find real locals, real history, and some of the most scenic walks in all of England — often without another tourist in sight.

Eastern Cotswold

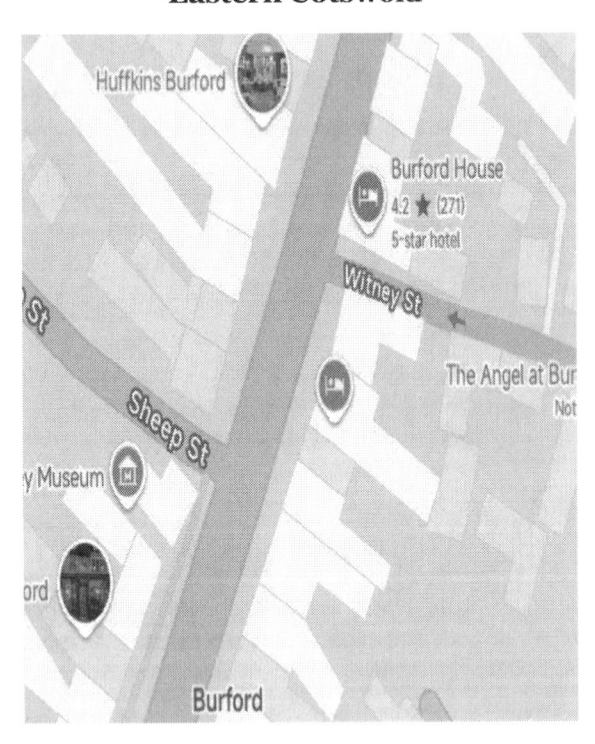

Burford – The Gateway to the Cotswolds with Medieval Soul

Burford is often called the Gateway to the Cotswolds, and that's no empty title. Located on the edge of Oxfordshire, right where the flat Thames Valley begins to roll into the Cotswold Hills, it serves as both a physical and emotional threshold between the bustle of modern England and the timeless charm of the Cotswolds. It's one of the oldest Cotswold towns, built on wool wealth, and its medieval character is still perfectly preserved.

The town's high street tumbles gently downhill, lined with 17th and 18th-century buildings in soft honey-colored stone. There's a slow rhythm to Burford — you hear it in the creak of shop doors, smell it in the woodsmoke and bread, and feel it when standing quietly in the shadow of its ancient church. It's popular, yes, but never brash — more of a connoisseur's stop than a casual photo-op. Burford rewards travelers who take time to linger.

Why Go: What Makes Burford Special?

What sets Burford apart is its blend of authentic history, working high street, and proximity to natural and cultural highlights. It feels like a real town, not a museum. You can browse antique shops, pick up local cheese at a proper deli, then stroll down to the Windrush River for a peaceful riverside moment.

Burford is also the perfect base for exploring both the Cotswolds and nearby Oxfordshire villages like Bampton (of Downton Abbey fame) or the wildlife-rich Cotswold Wildlife Park, just 5 minutes outside town. Whether you're into heritage churches, slow pub lunches, independent shopping, or scenic walks, Burford delivers — and it's especially magical outside peak summer, when the streets grow quieter and the mist settles on the hills.

How to Get There

- **From London:** Trains from London Paddington to Charlbury or Kingham (both about 1h15m–1h30m, £30–£45 return). From there, a taxi to Burford takes around 20–25 minutes and costs £25–£35.

- **By Car:** About 1 hour 45 minutes from London, via the M40 and A40. From

Oxford, it's only a 35-minute drive. Parking in town is free along the high street or behind the Co-op (limited).

- **Bus from Oxford:** Stagecoach bus S2 runs from Oxford to Burford, taking about 1h 10m and costing around £7–£10 one-way. It's practical for day-trippers.

Things to See & Do in Burford

- Burford High Street is a destination in itself. Pop into The Oxford Shirt Company, Huffkins Tea Room, or The Sweet Shop for proper handmade fudge. Window shopping here is a pleasure.

- St. John the Baptist Church is a must. This 12th-century church was once the wealthiest in the area, with royal connections and Civil War graffiti in the side chapel. Entry is free; donations welcome.

- Tolsey Museum, in a Tudor merchant house, gives you a bite-sized local history lesson. Free to enter, open spring to autumn.

- Burford Garden Company is 5 minutes outside town and one of the most stylish garden/home lifestyle shops in the UK. It has a beautiful café, too. Plan for £15–£25 for lunch, or more if you get tempted by the artisan goods inside.

Where to Eat

- **Huffkins Café & Bakery:** An institution since 1890, with cream teas, sausage rolls, and proper scones (cream tea from £8.50).
- **The Highway Inn:** Fantastic lunch spot and wine list (mains from £16–£25). Also offers rooms.
- **Spice Lounge:** If you want a break from pub food, this small Indian restaurant is surprisingly good and affordable (mains around £10–£14).

Where to Stay

- **The Lamb Inn** – This 15th-century former weaver's cottage is a luxurious but relaxed place to stay, with low beams, open fires, and a lovely garden. Rooms from £150–£220 per night, but worth it for the ambience and location.
- **The Bay Tree Hotel** – Just off the high street, this ivy-clad manor house is romantic and ideal for couples. Prices from £140–£180 depending on the season.
- **Burford Lodge** – A more affordable B&B option just outside the center, with rooms starting at £95. Friendly staff and good parking.

Practical Tips & Costs

- **Best Time to Visit:** Spring (April–May) and autumn (late September–early November) offer the best balance of beauty and quiet. Summer weekends get crowded with day-trippers.
- **Daily Budget Estimate (Mid-range):**
    - **Accommodation:** £120
    - **Food & Drink:** £35–£50
    - **Transport (if car hire):** £40 per day with fuel
    - **Attractions/Shopping:** £15–£30
    - **Total/day:** Approx. £180–£240

If you're on a tighter budget, go for off-season, take public transport, and stay in nearby Witney or Carterton, where B&Bs are around £70–£90 per night and you can bus into Burford easily.

Final Thoughts

Burford is not just a place to pass through — it's a place to stay a while and absorb. It has genuine historic depth, modern comforts, and a lived-in warmth that makes it stand apart from postcard-pretty but sterile spots. Whether you're looking for a weekend getaway, a stop on a longer Cotswolds itinerary, or a base to explore the eastern side of the region, Burford is as practical as it is picturesque.

Witney – Market Town with Local Soul

Witney is one of the most practical and livable market towns on the eastern fringe of the Cotswolds, located about 12 miles west of Oxford. It's not always included on the average Cotswolds itinerary because it lacks the "chocolate-box" look of villages like Bourton or Bibury — but that's exactly why it deserves a closer look.

Historically, Witney was famed for its wool and blanket-making industry, and the remnants of that past still influence its layout — from wide market streets to grand mills converted into flats and shops. Today, it's a working town with a relaxed feel, excellent local pubs, modern amenities, and easy transport links. It also has the advantage of being significantly more affordable than many of the Cotswolds hotspots.

Why Go to Witney?

If you're looking for a budget-friendly base with good access to the rest of the region, Witney is ideal. It's well-connected, has great restaurants, a bustling Thursday and Saturday market, and offers a glimpse of real English life. There's plenty of green space, too — The Leys is a great central park, and the Windrush Path offers riverside walks that feel very "Cotswold" without the tourist rush.

Travel from London:

Take a train from London Paddington to Oxford (around 1 hour, £25–£35), then a direct Stagecoach S1 or S2 bus from Oxford to Witney. The bus ride takes about 35–40 minutes and costs £6–£10. Witney is also accessible by car — about 1 hour 45 minutes from London via the M40 and A40.

Costs:

Accommodation in Witney is very reasonable compared to central Cotswolds locations. You'll find guesthouses like Corncroft Guest House and The Fleece offering rooms from £85–£120 per night with breakfast. Meals at pubs or restaurants range from £10–£25 per main, and you can shop at local bakeries, markets, and cafés for cheaper meals.

Charlbury – Hidden Countryside Gem with a Railway Link

Charlbury is one of my personal favourites in the Cotswolds — a small, charming town nestled in the Evenlode Valley, surrounded by ancient forest and classic stone cottages, yet with a direct rail line from Oxford and London. It feels like a secret, with fewer tourists and a relaxed, friendly vibe.

Despite its modest size, Charlbury has real depth: historic buildings, beautiful woodland walks, and a strong sense of community. It's also just minutes from Cornbury Park, one of the grandest estates in Oxfordshire, known for festivals like Wilderness. There's something timeless about Charlbury — and it's a place where you feel more like a guest than a tourist.

Why Go to Charlbury?

56

If you want to experience the Cotswolds slowly, surrounded by locals, dog walkers, and artisan food producers rather than coach tours, Charlbury is the place. It's perfect for walkers — the Cotswold Line brings you directly into town, and the surrounding countryside is part of the Wychwood Forest, a former royal hunting ground with ancient oaks and peaceful trails.

Travel from London:

Direct trains from London Paddington to Charlbury run via the Cotswold Line, operated by GWR. Journey time is around 1 hour 15 minutes and costs £30–£45 return, depending on the time of day and booking class. Charlbury station is just a short walk from the village centre.

Where to Stay:

- **The Bull Inn** — Beautiful rooms above a stylish pub. Expect £130–£180 per night, with modern rustic design and great food.
- **Cotswolds Camping at Holycombe** — For something quirky, you can stay in eco-pods or bell tents just outside Charlbury from £50–£90 per night.

Food & Drink:

- The Bull and The Rose & Crown are top picks for pub meals, both with hearty dishes from £14–£25 per main and local ale.
- A small Co-op and local bakeries mean you can self-cater affordably, especially if staying in an Airbnb or inn.

Charlbury vs. Witney – Which Should You Choose?

Choose Charlbury if you're seeking serenity, nature, and good rail access, with a strong local feel. It's ideal for walkers, writers, or anyone needing a quiet, soulful base.

Choose Witney if you want more shops, restaurants, nightlife, and affordability, while still being within 30–40 minutes of the classic Cotswold villages. It's a good hub for day-trips to Burford, Minster Lovell, and the Cotswold Wildlife Park.

Final Thought

Both Witney and Charlbury prove that the eastern Cotswolds aren't just gateways — they're destinations in their own right. You don't need to spend hundreds a night in a manor house to enjoy the region. With clever planning, you can stay affordably, eat well, and explore authentically, all while enjoying easy transport links and a more grounded, local experience of the Cotswolds.

Swinbrook – Literary Legacy and Riverside Peace

Tucked away just 2 miles east of Burford, Swinbrook is the kind of village you only find when you're either lost or guided by someone who truly knows the area. It's extraordinarily peaceful — a small cluster of honey-stone cottages straddling a winding country lane, bordered by water meadows and the gentle River Windrush. There's no souvenir shop, no queues, and certainly no crowds. Just timeless beauty.

What makes Swinbrook exceptional is its authenticity and literary heritage. This was the childhood home of the famous Mitford sisters, an aristocratic family whose lives and writings were woven into the social and political fabric of 20th-century England. Their graves lie in the quiet, moss-covered churchyard of St. Mary's Church, beside the village's famous "Fettiplace monuments" — beautifully carved Renaissance-era tombs inside the church.

Why Go to Swinbrook?

Go for quiet countryside walks, riverside picnics, and one of the best, most atmospheric pubs in the Cotswolds. If you're tracing the literary and aristocratic veins of British history, this village is a small but significant stop. Swinbrook is also a perfect base or detour from Burford (5 minutes' drive or a 45-minute riverside walk via footpath).

Where to Eat:

The Swan Inn is the village's heart and highlight. Set on the riverbank and run by the Daylesford group, it offers classic but refined Cotswold fare — think seasonal pies, fresh local veg, and hearty roasts. Expect mains from £18–£28, and a warm, fire-lit pub atmosphere in colder months. You can also stay overnight: rooms upstairs go for £130–£160 per night, including breakfast.

How to Get There:

- **By Car:** From Burford, it's a 5-minute drive or a pleasant 2-mile walk via bridleways and fields.
- **By Public Transport:** Swinbrook itself isn't on a bus line. The nearest bus stop is Burford (via Stagecoach S2 or 233 from Witney or Oxford), then a taxi (£10–£12) or walk.

Asthall – Woodland Trails and Sculpture Among the Stones

Just 2 miles from Swinbrook lies Asthall, another riverside hamlet with a haunting beauty all its own. It's most famous for Asthall Manor, a private Jacobean house that was also home to the Mitford sisters in the early 20th century. Today, it opens periodically to host "on form", a world-class sculpture exhibition held every other summer (next one: 2026), where contemporary stone sculptures are displayed throughout the house and gardens.

The village itself is barely more than a handful of stone homes and farms, all scattered along the narrow Asthall Road. It's backed by thick woods and sits directly on the Oxfordshire Way, a long-distance footpath that gives Asthall an almost hidden, discovered-on-foot vibe.

Why Go to Asthall?

Asthall is for those who love quiet walks, wildflowers, literary echoes, and art in unexpected places. It's close enough to be visited in conjunction with Swinbrook or Burford but secluded enough to feel like a true discovery. When on form is running (usually June–July), the manor grounds come alive with art lovers and picnickers. Outside those times, you'll likely have the paths and lanes to yourself.

Costs and Logistics:

- Entry to the form is usually around £10–£15 per adult (book in advance).
- Accommodation options are limited in Asthall, but nearby Swinbrook, Burford, and Witney offer excellent stays ranging from £90–£150 per night.

Getting There:

- By Car: It's 5 minutes from Swinbrook or 10 minutes from Burford via A40.
- **By Public Transport:** Like Swinbrook, Asthall is best accessed by car or on foot. Walking from Burford or Swinbrook takes about 45–60 minutes, mostly through countryside footpaths.

Walking Routes Between the Villages

One of the best ways to enjoy Swinbrook and Asthall is on foot. Park or stay in Burford, then take a leisurely 4–5 mile loop via the Windrush Valley footpaths. The trail follows the river, cuts through meadows, and gives you a deep sense of the land's rhythm. It's easy to moderate, with gentle slopes and plenty of picnic spots. Bring water and good shoes — the paths can get muddy after rain.

Final Thought

Swinbrook and Asthall are not bucket-list destinations — and that's their superpower. They're the kind of places that whisper their charm rather than shout it. If you want the Cotswolds without the crowds, with stories behind the stone and history underfoot, then these villages are absolutely worth your time. They're best enjoyed slowly, ideally with a long walk, a good meal, and a quiet evening in a nearby pub.

Western Cotswold & Outskirts

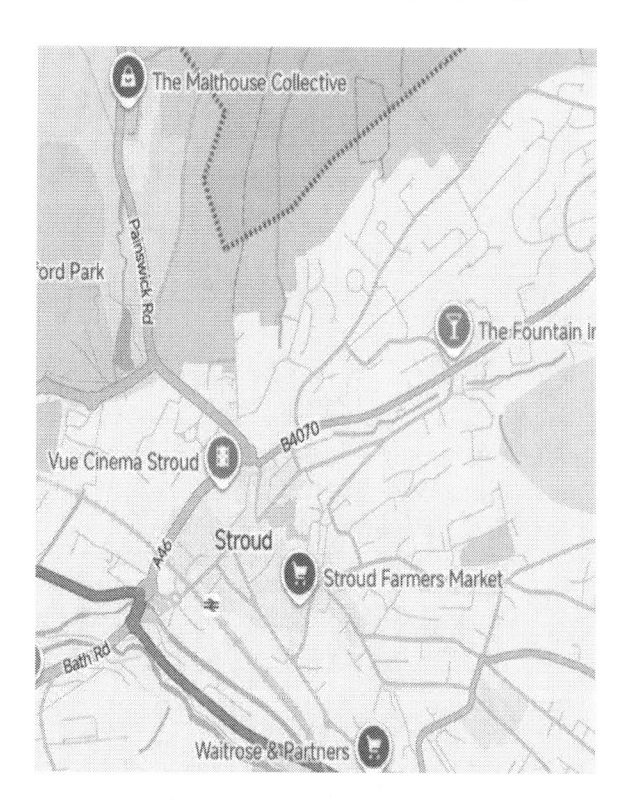

Stroud – The Bohemian Soul of the Western Cotswolds

Stroud is unlike any other town in the Cotswolds. Nestled in a bowl of five verdant valleys in the westernmost edge of the region, it has a raw, creative spirit, a fiercely independent streak, and a genuine, lived-in charm that sets it apart from its more picture-perfect Cotswold cousins like Bibury or Bourton-on-the-Water.

It's a place you visit not to admire from behind a camera lens, but to experience: bustling farmers' markets, eccentric indie shops, restored woollen mills, woodland hikes, and a vibrant arts and crafts culture that goes back to the Industrial Revolution and lives on in full color today.

Why Visit Stroud?

Stroud is where the Cotswolds collide with counterculture. Once a major hub for the wool trade, the town is now a magnet for artists, eco-entrepreneurs, and those seeking an alternative way of life. It's particularly beloved by those who want a local, grassroots, and sustainable experience, rather than a polished tourist postcard.

The Stroud Farmers' Market, held every Saturday in the town centre, is easily one of the best in the UK — a feast of organic produce, street food, handmade goods, artisan cheeses, sourdough, Cotswold cider, and even vegan baklava. Expect to spend around £15–£20 for a good lunch or grocery bag, and trust me, it's worth every pound.

But Stroud is also about landscape: the surrounding valleys — Slad, Painswick, Nailsworth, Chalford and Ruscombe — are laced with hiking trails, historic mills, and hidden woodland cafes. The Laurie Lee Wildlife Way, which loops around the Slad Valley, is one of the finest literary and nature trails in England, tracing the footsteps of the poet Laurie Lee who immortalized the area in Cider with Rosie. It's a free, self-guided walk (10 miles, moderate difficulty) and ideal for a spring or autumn day.

Cost of Visiting & Staying in Stroud

Stroud is generally more affordable than the central Cotswolds, making it a great base for budget-conscious travelers who still want local character. You'll find:

- Boutique B&Bs and eco-lodges from around £75–£120 per night.
- Airbnbs and apartments from £65–£110 per night, especially in the surrounding valleys.
- The Clothiers Arms, a cozy pub with rooms, offers stays from £90 including breakfast — a local favourite.

Eating out can be very reasonable. Try Falafel Mama for street food (£5–£7 wraps), Woodruffs Café for organic brunch (£8–£12), or The Prince Albert up the hill for live music and a great Sunday roast (£16–£19). For a mid-range sit-down dinner, expect around £25–£35 per person including drinks.

How to Get to Stroud

Stroud is well-connected despite feeling like it's off the tourist trail.

- **From London Paddington:** Take a direct train via Great Western Railway (about 1h 35m, costs £25–£45 return if booked in advance).
- **From Bristol Temple Meads:** Direct train, around 40 minutes, fare around £10–£18.
- **By car:** Stroud is just off the A46, about 30 minutes from Cheltenham, 40 minutes from Bristol, and 15–20 minutes from Cirencester.

Parking in town is manageable — Stratford Park Car Park and Merrywalks multi-storey are good central choices, with rates around £2–£4 per day.

Things to Do in and Around Stroud

- **Stroud Farmers' Market (Saturdays)** – Don't miss it. Truly among the UK's best.
- **Museum in the Park** – A small but excellent local museum showcasing Stroud's textile and social history. Free entry.
- **Woodchester Mansion** – A hauntingly beautiful unfinished Gothic revival house in the woods, entry around £9.
- **Walking the Five Valleys** – Free and spectacular; the Slad Valley is the most iconic.
- **Explore Slad** – Visit Laurie Lee's grave, have a pint at The Woolpack Inn with panoramic valley views.

Who Is Stroud Best For?

Stroud is ideal if you're into:

- Local food, organic living, and farmers' markets.
- Alternative arts and a creative vibe.
- Long walks in quiet, untamed countryside.
- Vintage shops, independent bookshops, and social enterprises.
- Literary history, particularly the life of Laurie Lee.

It's less polished than villages like Broadway or Stow-on-the-Wold, but that's the beauty of it. You come to Stroud for connection, not curation — to taste and walk and chat with real locals.

Final Word

To truly understand the Cotswolds, you must include Stroud in your journey. It balances out the romantic prettiness of the other towns with something earthier, realer, and more alive. For many repeat visitors (myself included), Stroud ends up being not just a detour, but a destination that quietly steals your heart.

Berkeley – A Step Back into Medieval and Tudor England

Berkeley is one of those quintessentially English small towns that feels like a living history book. Nestled on the western edge of the Cotswolds, close to the Severn Estuary, Berkeley is most famous for Berkeley Castle, a well-preserved medieval fortress that has been the home of the Berkeley family for over 850 years. This alone makes it a must-visit for anyone interested in English history, architecture, or heritage.

The castle's highlights include its magnificent Great Hall, original medieval kitchens, and beautiful gardens, all set within defensive stone walls and surrounded by a moat. Guided tours (usually about £14.50 for adults, £7.25 for children) are available from April through October, offering fascinating insights into British royal history—most notably, Berkeley Castle is where King Edward II was allegedly imprisoned and murdered in 1327. This link to royal intrigue adds a palpable sense of drama and mystery to your visit.

Berkeley's village itself is peaceful, with traditional stone cottages and a few local pubs. The White Lion Inn is a recommended spot to enjoy traditional pub fare with local ales at reasonable prices (main courses from £12–£18). It's a perfect place to wind down after exploring the castle and the surrounding countryside.

For travelers coming from London, the easiest route is by car or train. Berkeley is roughly a 2-hour drive (about 100 miles) southwest of London via the M4 and A38. There is no direct train station in Berkeley itself, but nearby Sharpness station is used primarily for freight, so most travelers take a train to Gloucester or Cam & Dursley and then catch a local taxi or bus. Bus services are limited; a taxi from Gloucester or Dursley will cost approximately £15–£25 depending on distance.

Dursley – A Vibrant Market Town with Modern Charm

Just a few miles east of Berkeley lies Dursley, a larger market town that mixes traditional Cotswold charm with modern amenities. Unlike the tourist-centric villages, Dursley is a lively commercial and residential hub serving the local community, which gives visitors a genuine feel of daily life in the Cotswolds beyond the postcard villages.

Dursley's high street offers a range of independent shops, cafes, and essential services, with prices that are moderate and fair. For budget travelers, there are plenty of affordable eateries and takeaways where a meal can cost as little as £7–£10, and supermarkets like Tesco and Aldi provide options for self-catering.

One of Dursley's key draws is its excellent rail connectivity. The Dursley railway station, on the Bristol–Gloucester line, offers regular services to Bristol (about 30 minutes), Gloucester (10 minutes), and direct trains to London Paddington (typically around 2 hours with one change). Tickets booked in advance can cost as low as £15 one-way to Bristol or £35–£50 return to London. This makes Dursley a great base for those who want to explore the Cotswolds while having easy access to larger cities.

For outdoor lovers, Dursley is close to the Cotswold Way National Trail, with several accessible walking routes starting near the town that traverse beautiful limestone hills and valleys. Nearby Stinchcombe Hill is a local favorite for panoramic views and is free to visit.

Accommodations in Dursley range from budget B&Bs starting around £50–£70 per night to comfortable hotels like The Kingshill House Hotel, where rooms typically cost £90–£120 per night. These are excellent options for travelers who want to enjoy the Cotswolds with fewer crowds and more authentic local life.

Why Visit Berkeley and Dursley Together?

Berkeley and Dursley complement each other perfectly for a well-rounded experience of the western Cotswolds. Berkeley provides history and heritage steeped in centuries of English tradition, while Dursley offers modern convenience, connectivity, and a glimpse into contemporary Cotswold life. Both are less touristy than central Cotswold hotspots, allowing for a quieter, more authentic visit.

From a practical standpoint, traveling between these two towns is easy and quick by car (around 10 minutes via the B4066) or by local bus, though bus services can be sparse. They are both well placed for day trips into the wider Cotswolds, the Forest of Dean, and the Severn Estuary coastline.

In Summary:

- **Berkeley Castle:** A highlight, £14.50 entry, open Apr-Oct, deep historical significance.
- **Dursley Station:** Great transport links, affordable accommodation, local shops, and eateries.
- **Travel Tips:** Car hire is recommended for full flexibility; expect to spend £30–£40/day on car rental plus fuel.
- **Dining:** Traditional pub meals around £12–£18; casual eateries and takeaways in Dursley from £7.
- **Accommodation:** B&Bs and hotels range from £50–£120 per night depending on style and season.

If you enjoy history, authentic local culture, and a mix of peaceful village life with convenient transport, Berkeley and Dursley make a compelling, practical, and very enjoyable pair to include in your Cotswolds itinerary.

Day Trips to Gloucester & Cheltenham

Having explored the Cotswolds multiple times, I can confidently say that taking day trips to Gloucester and Cheltenham offers a wonderful contrast to the rural charm of the region, blending history, culture, and vibrant urban life within easy reach. Both towns are rich in character and easily accessible, making them ideal for anyone looking to diversify their Cotswolds experience beyond the quintessential villages.

Gloucester is just about 20 miles west of the central Cotswolds and stands out for its remarkable medieval cathedral, which is arguably one of the most stunning in England. The cathedral's magnificent fan-vaulted ceilings, cloisters, and stained-glass windows are a highlight for any visitor, especially fans of architecture or history buffs. It also famously appeared as a filming location for the Harry Potter movies, which adds a modern cultural allure. Entry to Gloucester Cathedral is free, though donations are appreciated to help maintain the site.

Besides the cathedral, Gloucester offers a lively historic docks area, fully transformed into a waterside destination packed with cafes, pubs, and boutique shops. Strolling along the docks feels cosmopolitan but relaxed—perfect for lunch or afternoon tea. Expect to spend around £10-£15 for a good meal in a dockside eatery. For history lovers, Gloucester's Museum of Gloucester (free entry) showcases Roman artifacts and local history, providing insight into the city's evolution from Roman times to today.

Getting to Gloucester is straightforward. From central Cotswolds towns like Cheltenham or Moreton-in-Marsh, you can take a direct train; for example, Cheltenham to Gloucester is just a quick 15-minute train ride costing about £5–£7 one way when booked in advance. From London, Gloucester is roughly a 2-hour train journey with prices ranging from £25 to £50 return depending on timing and advance booking.

About Cheltenham, often called the "Gateway to the Cotswolds," it is a lively Regency town known for its elegant architecture, festivals, and cultural scene. Cheltenham's broad, tree-lined avenues and historic buildings create a sophisticated atmosphere that contrasts beautifully with the rural villages.

The town is famous for its literature and jazz festivals, drawing crowds each year, but even outside festival times, Cheltenham has plenty to offer. The Cheltenham Art Gallery and Museum (free entry) houses local art, natural history, and exhibits on Cheltenham's spa heritage, which dates back to the 18th century when it became a fashionable health resort.

Shopping is a draw here, with a mix of high-street brands, independent boutiques, and artisan markets. For foodies, Cheltenham offers everything from cozy tea rooms serving traditional cream teas (around £5–£7 per person) to high-end restaurants where a three-course meal can range from £30 to £50. A popular local dining experience is trying a classic Cotswold lamb dish or sampling seasonal local produce.

Travel to Cheltenham from the Cotswolds is also convenient. If you are in Moreton-in-Marsh, there are direct trains to Cheltenham Spa station taking about 30 minutes and costing around £8–£12 one way. By car, Cheltenham is easily reached via the A40 or A417, typically within a 30 to 45-minute drive from central Cotswold villages like Bourton-on-the-Water or Stow-on-the-Wold.

Practical Tips:

For day trippers, combining Gloucester and Cheltenham in a single day is doable but better split over two days to fully appreciate each town. A car rental offers the most flexibility, with typical daily rates around £30–£40, but good train links make public transport a viable and cost-effective option. Taxi fares between Cheltenham and Gloucester hover around £25–£35 if you prefer direct, private transfer.

Parking in both towns is available but can be costly and busy, especially during festivals—expect £2–£4 per hour in central areas. Arriving early in the morning or using park-and-ride facilities on the outskirts is a good way to avoid hassle.

Why Go?

- Gloucester offers deep historical roots and a revitalized urban waterfront, perfect for those who want history plus modern vibes.

- Cheltenham provides a polished cultural experience, with shopping, dining, and festivals that add vibrancy to the Cotswolds visit.

- Both are easily accessible by train or car, making them practical day trip choices without needing to leave the Cotswolds region.

Visiting Gloucester and Cheltenham enriches your Cotswolds trip by layering in urban exploration, history, and contemporary British culture, all within a reasonable budget and travel distance. Whether you choose to explore the medieval grandeur of Gloucester Cathedral or soak up Cheltenham's elegant Regency charm, these day trips are a perfect complement to the pastoral beauty and quaint villages of the Cotswolds.

Walking and hiking in the Cotswolds is one of the most immersive ways to experience the region's timeless charm. With its rolling hills, honey-stone villages, hidden valleys, and sweeping countryside vistas, the Cotswolds is a walker's paradise — and it caters to all levels, from casual strollers to long-distance hikers. Having explored these trails over multiple visits, I can say each path offers something distinct: historical landmarks, postcard-worthy views, and a pace of travel that connects you intimately with the land.

Chapter 4 : Experiences & Themes

Walking & Hiking Trails

The Cotswold Way

This is the crown jewel of long-distance walking in the region — a 102-mile National Trail stretching from Chipping Campden in the north to the historic city of Bath in the south. If you're serious about walking, doing all or part of the Cotswold Way is an unforgettable journey.

Expect to pass through market towns like Broadway, Winchcombe, Painswick, and Dursley, along with ancient woodlands, hill forts like Belas Knap, and the spectacular views from Cleeve Hill, the highest point in the Cotswolds.

- **Difficulty:** Moderate. It includes a number of ascents and descents but is well-signposted.
- **Time Required:** About 7–10 days to complete the full trail.
- **Cost:** Free to walk; accommodation along the way (B&Bs, inns, or hostels) averages £60–£120 per night. Luggage transfer services like Cotswold Walks or Sherpa Van can be booked for around £10–£15 per bag/day.
- **Best For:** Serious walkers wanting a full immersion into the Cotswolds' landscapes, heritage sites, and rural charm.

The Windrush Way

This lesser-known but deeply rewarding trail stretches 13 miles between Bourton-on-the-Water and Winchcombe. It's an excellent one-day walk that takes you across quiet farmland, wooded hills, and gentle river valleys, following the course of the River Windrush for much of the way.

- **Difficulty:** Easy to Moderate.
- **Time Required:** 5–6 hours at a comfortable pace.
- **Cost:** Free; just pack your own picnic or stop in Bourton or Winchcombe for a pub lunch (~£10–£15).
- **Route Tip:** Start from Winchcombe for an early lunch in Bourton-on-the-Water (ample café options), then take a local taxi or bus back (budget £12–£20 for a taxi; buses are less frequent so check local timetables in advance).
- **Best For:** Day walkers who want a tranquil countryside ramble with rich scenery and fewer crowds.

Local Circular Walks

The Cotswolds is riddled with local footpaths and circular trails that link charming villages, historic churches, meadows, and woodlands — all with public access. These short-to-moderate loops are ideal if you're based in one village and want to explore the surroundings without needing transport.

Some of the best include:

- **The Slaughters Circular:** Starting in Lower Slaughter, this 3–5 mile loop connects Upper Slaughter and Bourton-on-the-Water, following the River Eye. Gentle terrain, iconic views, and easily walkable in 2–3 hours.

- **Painswick to Slad Valley Loop:** This 6-mile loop combines the idyllic charm of Painswick with stunning views over the Slad Valley — Laurie Lee country. Expect moderate inclines, open pastures, and wooded paths. Allow about 3.5 hours.

- **Blockley to Batsford Arboretum Loop:** A 5-mile route from the charming village of Blockley through fields and forest tracks to the Batsford Arboretum (entry ~£9.50), making it a rewarding half-day walk.

- **Broadway Tower Walk:** A 4-mile loop from Broadway village up to Broadway Tower, the second-highest point in the Cotswolds. Entry to the tower is £14 for adults, or you can simply enjoy the surrounding parkland. It's moderately steep and takes about 2 hours round trip.

- **Stow-on-the-Wold to Maugersbury Circular:** An easy 2.5-mile stroll that offers gorgeous rural views and easy terrain — perfect for families or casual walkers. Takes about 1.5 hours.

Most circular walks are free, and downloadable route maps are available via Cotswolds AONB website or Ordnance Survey apps. Signposting is usually good, but a printed or digital map is advisable.

Practical Tips

- **Footwear:** Waterproof hiking shoes or sturdy trainers are a must — some routes get muddy, even in summer.
- **Maps:** The OS Explorer maps (OL45 for North Cotswolds and OL168 for South) are incredibly helpful.
- **Weather:** Always check the forecast. Even in summer, sudden rain showers can turn a trail slick.
- **Safety:** Mobile reception is patchy in remote spots; download maps offline and carry water, especially in summer.
- **Dogs:** Most walks are dog-friendly but keep dogs on leads near livestock.

Why Go Walking in the Cotswolds?

Walking in the Cotswolds gives you access to the hidden layers of the region — stone stile footpaths tucked between drystone walls, old Roman roads, and paths trodden by farmers and poets for centuries. You can walk straight from your inn door to the hills, and many walks end (or begin) at a traditional pub, making it a uniquely satisfying and accessible experience. Whether you spend a morning walking from Bourton to the Slaughters or commit to the full Cotswold Way, these trails are the heart and soul of Cotswold travel.

Gardens, Manor Houses & Historic Sites

Hidcote Manor, Sudeley Castle, Blenheim Palace

Exploring the gardens, manor houses, and historic estates of the Cotswolds is essential to truly understanding the region's blend of aristocratic heritage, natural beauty, and horticultural innovation. From carefully curated Arts and Crafts gardens to grand palaces tied to British royalty, the Cotswolds is home to some of the most iconic and well-preserved estates in England. Here's a practical, in-depth look at three standout destinations: Hidcote Manor Garden, Sudeley Castle, and Blenheim Palace — each offering distinct experiences worth your time and budget.

Hidcote Manor Garden (Near Chipping Campden)

Hidcote is one of the most influential gardens in England, and certainly among the most famous in the Cotswolds. Located just a 10-minute drive northeast of Chipping Campden, this National Trust property is a masterpiece of 20th-century garden design. Created by American horticulturist Major Lawrence Johnston in the early 1900s, it pioneered the "garden room" concept — with a series of outdoor spaces enclosed by hedges, each with its own theme, colour palette, and planting style.

- **Why Go:** For gardening enthusiasts, Hidcote is a pilgrimage site. The Red Border, White Garden, and Fuchsia Garden showcase rare plants and clever spatial design. Even for casual visitors, the layout is mesmerizing, with hidden alcoves and unexpected views around every corner.
- **Best Time to Visit:** Late spring to early summer (May–July) for peak blooms.
- **Opening Hours:** Daily, 10am–5pm (seasonal variations apply).
- **Cost:** Adults £16, Children £8, or free for National Trust members.
- **Tips:** Arrive early to avoid crowds, especially in peak season. Combine with a trip to Kiftsgate Court Gardens (just next door), another hidden gem run by three generations of women gardeners.
- **Public Transport:** Nearest rail station is Moreton-in-Marsh; from there, a taxi (~£18–£22) is the most direct route.

Sudeley Castle (Winchcombe)

Steeped in over 1,000 years of history, Sudeley Castle is not just a beautifully preserved Tudor residence — it's a rare historic site still used as a family home. Located just outside the village of Winchcombe, it is best known as the final resting place of Queen Katherine Parr, the last wife of Henry VIII, who is buried in the castle's charming chapel.

- **Why Go:** The combination of romantic ruins, lush gardens (10 themed gardens in total), and accessible Tudor history make Sudeley a standout. The Queens' Garden, where four English queens are said to have walked, bursts with roses in the summer. Inside the castle,

66

interactive exhibits and antique collections provide insight into its royal past.

- **Best Time to Visit:** Spring and early autumn for gardens and lighter crowds.
- **Opening Hours:** Typically March to October, Sun–Thu, 10am–5pm.
- **Cost:** Adults £19.50, Children (3–15) £8.75. Family ticket (2+2) £52. Discounts often available online.
- **Extras:** The café offers local food and cream teas (~£7–£12). The on-site pheasantry, housing rare birds, is a hit with kids.
- **Public Transport:** Bus service from Cheltenham to Winchcombe runs regularly, or a taxi from Moreton-in-Marsh costs around £25–£30.

Blenheim Palace (Woodstock, Eastern Edge of the Cotswolds)

Blenheim Palace is a UNESCO World Heritage Site and the birthplace of Sir Winston Churchill — and it's every bit as grand as its title suggests. Located in Woodstock, just outside the official Cotswolds boundary but still considered part of its orbit, Blenheim is an ideal day trip from Oxford or northern Cotswold villages like Burford or Charlbury.

- **Why Go:** With over 2,000 acres of Capability Brown–landscaped parkland, a jaw-dropping Baroque palace, formal gardens, and Churchill memorabilia, Blenheim offers a full day of culture, history, and walking. It's one of the finest examples of English stately grandeur.
- **Highlights:** Don't miss the State Rooms, the Churchill Exhibition, and a walk around the lake to the Grand Cascade. The Marlborough Maze and miniature train are a hit with families.
- **Opening Hours:** Year-round, daily from 10am (park open earlier).
- **Cost:** Adults £38.50 (Palace, Park & Gardens), Children £22.50, with discounts for students, seniors, or online booking. Annual pass upgrade available for free if you agree to donate your ticket cost.
- **Dining:** There are several dining options onsite — the Orangery Restaurant is the most formal (expect to spend £20–£30 per person for lunch).
- **Public Transport:** Frequent bus service from Oxford to Woodstock (S3 or 7), ~35 minutes. Driving from Burford takes ~30 minutes.

Final Tips for Visiting Historic Sites in the Cotswolds

- **Buy in Advance:** Booking online often saves 10–15% on entry fees.
- **National Trust & English Heritage Memberships:** If you plan to visit multiple sites, these can offer excellent value.
- **Go Midweek:** Weekends in summer can be crowded — midweek mornings offer a quieter, more atmospheric experience.
- **Dress Accordingly:** These sites often involve outdoor walking, so wear sturdy shoes and bring layers.

Each of these places tells a different story — Hidcote embodies the art of gardening, Sudeley tells tales of Tudor queens and survival, and Blenheim showcases aristocratic excess on a national scale. Together, they form an essential circuit for history lovers and cultural travelers in the Cotswolds.

Food & Drink in the Cotswolds

Food and drink in the Cotswolds is a genuine highlight of the region—an experience woven from centuries-old farming traditions, outstanding local produce, and atmospheric venues that range from rustic stone pubs to elegant manor tearooms. Having eaten extensively across the region, I can confidently say the Cotswolds punches well above its weight when it comes to culinary offerings. From hearty pub roasts and award-winning cheeses to refined afternoon teas, here's a well-rounded, practical guide to where to eat, what to try, and how much to expect to spend.

Top Pubs in the Cotswolds

The Cotswolds is renowned for its country pubs, often housed in honey-stone buildings with roaring fireplaces and characterful interiors. Many of these serve locally sourced menus that rival city gastropubs.

- **The Wild Rabbit – Kingham**

  This is a Michelin-starred pub-with-rooms under the Daylesford group. Think oak beams, open fires, and exquisitely plated modern British dishes. The wild venison (£34) and Cotswold lamb saddle (£32) are standouts.

  - **Cost:** Mains £26–£40, tasting menu ~£80 pp.
  - **Booking:** Essential, especially weekends.

- **The Ebrington Arms – Ebrington (near Chipping Campden)**

  A classic village pub with a sophisticated twist. Known for its award-winning pies and locally brewed Yubby ale. Their steak & ale pie (£19) is worth the detour.

  - **Cost:** Mains £17–£24.
  - **Tip:** Stay overnight for a cosy pub stay with breakfast.

- **The Bell Inn – Selsley (near Stroud)**

  Outstanding views and a creative seasonal menu. They serve a lot of locally grown veg and foraged ingredients. The slow-roast pork belly (£24) is exceptional.

  - **Cost:** £18–£28 for mains.

Farm Shops & Local Produce

Farm shops are a huge part of the Cotswold food experience, offering everything from organic meats and cheeses to fresh produce, baked goods, and handmade preserves.

- **Daylesford Organic – near Kingham**

  The most famous farm shop in the Cotswolds, Daylesford is a destination in itself. The deli offers everything from truffle cheese to bone broth. There's also a restaurant and café serving healthy, upscale farm-to-table meals.

  - **Cost:** Sandwiches & light meals from £10–£16, groceries premium-priced.
  - **Open:** Daily 8am–8pm.

- **Stroud Farmers' Market – Every Saturday**

  One of the best in the country. You'll find organic meat, Cotswold cheeses, artisan breads, and seasonal produce. Try the locally famous Hobbs House

Bakery sourdough and a piping hot Gloucester Old Spot sausage bap (£5).

- **Time:** Saturday mornings until 2pm. Go early for best selection.

- **Jesse Smith Butchers & Farm Shop – Cirencester**

A reliable spot for quality meats, including dry-aged steaks, local game, and Cotswold lamb. They also sell prepared items like scotch eggs, pork pies, and quiches.

- **Tip:** Their Cotswold beef burger kits are excellent value.

Tearooms & Afternoon Tea

There are few better places in England to enjoy a proper afternoon tea than in the Cotswolds, where heritage buildings and countryside views set the perfect scene.

- **The Tea Set – Chipping Norton & Broadway**

  - A charming tea room with vintage décor and proper bone china. Their full afternoon tea (£23.95) includes finger sandwiches, fresh scones with clotted cream, and homemade cakes.

  - Reservations recommended at peak times.

- **Huffkins Bakery & Tearooms – Stow-on-the-Wold, Burford, Witney**

  - An old-school bakery brand founded in 1890. Their cream tea (£9.95) is great value and their Lardy Cake is a Cotswold classic—don't leave without trying it.

  - **Tip:** You can buy their jam and biscuits as gifts.

- **Barnsley House – near Cirencester**

  - For a luxury tea room experience in a manor house setting. Afternoon tea in the gardens (weather permitting) is truly special.

  - **Cost:** Afternoon tea £35–£45 per person, with prosecco option.

Local Specialties to Try

- **Cotswold Lamb** – Often reared on limestone hills; tender and flavorful. Common in spring and autumn menus.
- **Double & Single Gloucester Cheese** – Local staples, often featured on cheese boards or in dishes like cheese soufflé.
- **Cotswold Gold Rapeseed Oil** – Used by many local chefs, known for its nutty flavour and bright yellow colour.
- **Hobbs House Bakery** – From the Fabulous Baker Brothers, their sourdough and bread pudding are beloved.
- **Gloucester Old Spot Pork** – A heritage pig breed producing rich, marbled meat. Look for it in sausages, chops, and pies.
- **Tewkesbury Mustard** – A spicy horseradish-mustard blend made famous in medieval times, often served with roasts.

Final Tips

- **Budget-Friendly Meals:** Look for pub lunch deals or set menus (often ~£12–£16 for two courses).
- **Booking:** Always book ahead for top-rated pubs, especially Friday–Sunday.
- **Dietary Needs:** Most places now accommodate gluten-free and vegetarian/vegan diets, but call ahead to be sure in smaller villages.
- **Local Ales & Ciders:** Try beers from Hook Norton, Stroud Brewery, or Donnington Brewery, and local ciders like Perry's from Gloucestershire.

The food scene in the Cotswolds is proudly rooted in its agricultural heritage but has also evolved to include modern British cuisine with international flair. Whether you're nibbling on scones in a thatched tearoom or tucking into a gourmet pie beside a crackling fire, the experience is rich, warm, and deeply satisfying.

Market Towns & Artisan Shops

The market towns of the Cotswolds are the beating heart of its local economy and cultural life, especially for those seeking authentic experiences through weekly markets, antique treasure hunts, and high-quality artisan shopping. Having visited these towns repeatedly over the years, I can say without hesitation that exploring their markets and independent shops is one of the best ways to feel the spirit of the region. These towns aren't just for ticking off sightseeing lists—they're living, working communities where tradition meets creativity, and shopping becomes a deeply local, rewarding experience.

Weekly Markets: A Tradition Still Thriving

Almost every significant town in the Cotswolds hosts a weekly market, usually in the central square or historic marketplace, dating back centuries. These markets are fantastic for picking up local cheeses, meats, preserves, handmade soaps, flowers, fresh produce, and sometimes vintage finds.

- **Cirencester Market (Mon & Fri for general; Farmers' Market 2nd/4th Saturdays)**

  The largest market in the region, set in the historic Market Place in front of the parish church. Expect over 100 stalls on busy days. Highlights include organic honey from local beekeepers, venison from Cotswold estates, handcrafted wood items.

  - **Tip:** Farmers' Market Saturdays are the best for artisan food.
  - **Cost:** Free to browse; expect £3.50 for a local cheese wedge, £5–£10 for preserves, and £6–£12 for handmade soaps.

- **Stow-on-the-Wold Market (2nd Thursday of the month)**

  Set around the town's ancient square. A mix of craft, vintage, and local food producers. Great for picking up hand-knitted wool items or small batch chutneys.

  - **Tip:** Go early for antiques—dealers often arrive before 9am.

- **Stroud Farmers' Market (Every Saturday, 9am–2pm)**

  Possibly the most famous farmers' market in the Cotswolds, held in Cornhill Market Place. You'll find organic veg, artisan bread (try Salt Bakehouse), sustainable fish, cider, and even locally roasted coffee.

- **Cost:** Loaves from £3.50, cider £4 per bottle, hot food stalls £7–£10 per portion.
- **Atmosphere:** Lively, community-focused, with live music often present.

- **Chipping Campden Market (Occasional pop-ups, summer especially)**

  Though smaller and less frequent, the local markets here focus on handmade items, books, and local food. The Market Hall, run by the National Trust, is a great setting for craft events.

Antiques: Hidden Treasures in Historic Towns

The Cotswolds is an antiques lover's paradise, especially for those interested in vintage English pottery, rustic furniture, maps, rare books, and textiles. The scene is thriving in towns like Tetbury, Burford, and Stow-on-the-Wold.

- **Tetbury**

  Arguably the antiques capital of the Cotswolds. The town has over 20 antiques shops within walking distance, including the highly regarded Lorfords Antiques (open Mon–Sat) housed in a historic hangar on the outskirts.

  - **Expect:** Georgian furniture, 18th-century mirrors, architectural salvage.
  - **Price Range:** £40 for vintage tableware to £4,000+ for restored Regency pieces.

- **Stow-on-the-Wold**

  Known for high-end antiques. Tara Antiques Centre and Paul E. Smith Antiques are great stops. Expect serious collectors and well-curated inventory.

  - **Cost:** £25 for smaller items (e.g., vintage silver spoons), £500+ for larger pieces.

- **Burford**

  A smaller but charming scene—check out Burford Antiques Centre on the High Street and the Burford Garden Company for antiques mixed with lifestyle shopping.

  - **Tip:** Many shops close on Sundays or shut early, especially off-season.

Artisan Shops & Local Crafts

The Cotswolds is home to a growing community of independent artisans, making it a great region for buying ceramics, woollens, natural skincare, candles, and handmade furniture.

- **Cotswold Woollen Weavers – Filkins (near Burford)**

  A working mill that produces and sells beautiful wool products. Their throws and tweed jackets are especially popular.

  - **Cost:** Scarves from £25, blankets £60–£150, jackets upwards of £180.
  - **Bonus:** The small on-site museum is free and insightful.

- **New Brewery Arts – Cirencester**

  A craft centre with workshops and a gallery. You'll find local artisans working in ceramics, textiles, glass, and leather.

- o **Shop:** Sells handmade items and offers workshops (pottery class ~£40).
- o **Tip:** Check their schedule for drop-in experiences or short courses.

- **Cotswold Lavender – Snowshill (seasonal: June–Aug)**

  Not only beautiful to walk through, but they also sell pure lavender oils, handmade soaps, and bath products.
  - o **Cost:** Lavender oil £8.50+, gift sets from £15.
  - o Shop open year-round, even when fields aren't in bloom.

- **Fosse Gallery – Stow-on-the-Wold**

  A leading gallery for British contemporary art, representing both emerging and established artists. If you're looking to invest in original pieces, this is one of the best in the region.
  - o **Cost:** Original artworks from £400–£5,000+.

Final Tips for Market & Artisan Shopping in the Cotswolds

- **Cash & Card:** Many vendors now accept card, but it's always wise to carry some cash for smaller stalls or rural markets.
- **Parking:** Free in some smaller towns, pay-and-display in larger ones like Cirencester or Burford (~£1.20–£2 per hour).
- **Sundays:** Many markets and independent shops close or have shorter hours on Sundays—plan accordingly.
- **Shipping:** For antiques or large items, most reputable dealers offer nationwide and sometimes international shipping (ask in store).

Whether you're treasure-hunting in Tetbury, picking up raw honey at Stroud Market, or browsing hand-thrown pottery in a village craft shop, market towns and artisan stores give you a tangible connection to the Cotswolds' heritage and contemporary creativity. Come with a shopping bag—and maybe an extra suitcase.

Festivals & Seasonal Events (2025/2026 Calendar)

The Cotswolds' festival calendar is a vibrant tapestry of cultural, musical, and culinary events that span the entire year. Whether you're a music enthusiast, a food lover, or someone seeking unique local traditions, there's something for everyone. Here's an in-depth guide to the most notable festivals and seasonal events in the Cotswolds for 2025 and early 2026, including dates, locations, costs, and planning tips.

Music & Arts Festivals

Cheltenham Jazz Festival

- **Dates:** 30 April – 5 May 2025
- **Location:** Cheltenham, Gloucestershire
- **Why Go:** Experience a stellar lineup of jazz legends and emerging talents across various venues, including a free stage in Montpellier Gardens.
- **Cost:** Ticket prices vary by event; some free performances available.
- **Planning Tip:** Book accommodations early, as the festival attracts visitors nationwide.

Wilderness Festival

- **Dates:** 31 July – 3 August 2025
- **Location:** Cornbury Park, Oxfordshire
- **Why Go:** A four-day celebration of music, food, arts, and nature, featuring acts like Basement Jaxx and Supergrass.
- **Cost:** Ticket prices vary; check the official website for details.
- **Planning Tip:** Ideal for those seeking a blend of cultural enrichment and outdoor adventure.

Big Feastival

- **Dates:** 22 – 24 August 2025
- **Location:** Alex James' Farm, Kingham, Oxfordshire
- **Why Go:** Combines top-tier live music with gourmet food experiences in a family-friendly setting.
- **Cost:** Ticket prices vary; early booking recommended.
- **Planning Tip:** Perfect for families and food enthusiasts; consider camping options for a full experience.l

Cotswold Fest

- **Dates:** 25 – 27 July 2025
- **Location:** Cotswolds (specific venue TBA)
- **Why Go:** A laid-back weekend featuring local bands, family activities, and regional cuisine.
- **Cost:** Ticket prices vary; check the official website for updates.
- **Planning Tip:** Great for a relaxed, community-focused festival experience.

Traditional & Quirky Events

Cooper's Hill Cheese Rolling

- **Date:** 26 May 2025 (Spring Bank Holiday)
- **Location:** Cooper's Hill, near Gloucester
- **Why Go:** Witness or participate in the world-famous, adrenaline-fueled race chasing a wheel of cheese down a steep hill.
- **Cost:** Free to attend; arrive early for good viewing spots.
- **Planning Tip:** Not for the faint-hearted; wear suitable footwear and be prepared for crowds.

Cotswold Olimpicks

- **Date:** 6 June 2025
- **Location:** Dover's Hill, near Chipping Campden
- **Why Go:** A historic event featuring traditional games like shin-kicking and tug-of-war, culminating in a torchlit procession.
- **Cost:** Ticket prices vary; check the official website for details.
- **Planning Tip:** Embrace the local culture by participating or cheering on the competitors.

Seasonal Highlights

Cheltenham Literature Festival

- **Dates:** 3 – 12 October 2025
- **Location:** Cheltenham, Gloucestershire
- **Why Go:** Engage with renowned authors, attend readings, and participate in literary discussions.
- **Cost:** Ticket prices vary by event; some free sessions available.
- **Planning Tip:** Ideal for literature enthusiasts; book tickets early for popular sessions.

Christmas Markets

- **Dates:** Late November – December 2025
- **Locations:** Cheltenham, Cirencester, Gloucester, and other towns

- **Why Go:** Experience festive cheer with local crafts, seasonal foods, and holiday entertainment.
- **Cost:** Free entry; costs vary for goods and food.
- **Planning Tip:** Visit during weekdays to avoid weekend crowds.

Planning Your Visit

To make the most of these events:

- **Book Accommodations Early:** Festivals attract many visitors; securing lodging in advance ensures better options and rates.
- **Check Official Websites:** For the latest information on tickets, schedules, and any changes.
- **Consider Transportation:** Public transport may be limited in rural areas; plan accordingly.
- **Pack Appropriately:** Weather can be unpredictable; bring suitable clothing and footwear.

By aligning your travel plans with these vibrant festivals and events, you'll experience the Cotswolds' rich cultural tapestry in full bloom.

Literary, Arts & Film Locations

The Cotswolds is not only a region of honey-stoned villages and rolling countryside — it's also a rich literary and cinematic landscape that has inspired world-famous authors, served as the backdrop for beloved films and TV series, and continues to draw culture-seeking travelers. From the world of Downton Abbey to the poetic roots of Laurie Lee, and even the rumored inspirations for J.K. Rowling's magical universe, here's an in-depth guide to the Cotswolds' literary, arts, and film connections — including locations, what to see, costs, and how to get there.

Downton Abbey (Highclere Castle & Bampton)

- **Primary Filming Locations:**

    While Downton Abbey's main filming location — Highclere Castle — is just outside the official Cotswolds boundary in Hampshire (about a 45-minute drive south of Burford), much of the village life was shot in the Cotswold village of Bampton (Oxfordshire).

- **Why Go:**

  Bampton served as the fictional village of Downton. St Mary's Church, the old grammar school (used as the hospital), and Churchgate House are all instantly recognizable filming sites. The charm of the village is authentic and largely untouched.

- **Location & Getting There:**

  Bampton is located near Witney in Oxfordshire. It's accessible via car (around 30 minutes from Oxford), or by bus from Oxford's Gloucester Green Station to Bampton (about 1 hour via Stagecoach S1).

- **Costs:**

  Visiting Bampton is free. Entry to Highclere Castle (should you wish to see the manor itself) is £29–£36 per adult depending on the season and whether you book a guided tour or special event (www.highclere castle.co.uk).

- **Best Time to Visit:**

  Highclere Castle is only open for limited periods (mainly spring, summer, and Christmas events), so booking ahead is essential. Bampton can be visited year-round.

Laurie Lee's Slad Valley – "Cider with Rosie" Country

- **Why Go:**

  The village of Slad, near Stroud, is immortalized in Laurie Lee's evocative memoir Cider with Rosie, which captures rural life in the early 20th century. The landscape is unchanged — meadows, woodlands, stone cottages — offering a true step back in time.

- **What to See:**

  Walk the Laurie Lee Wildlife Way, a 5-mile circular walk with ten poetry posts featuring excerpts from Lee's works. Visit The Woolpack Inn, his beloved local pub, which retains its rustic charm and serves excellent local ales and food.

- **Location & Getting There:**

  Slad is just 10 minutes' drive from Stroud. You can also take a taxi (approx. £10–£15 from Stroud station). There's limited public transport.

- **Costs:**

  Free to visit. The walk is self-guided and well signposted. The Woolpack offers meals from around £15–£25 per person (www.the woolpack slad.com).

- **Best Time to Visit:**

  Late spring through early autumn offers the best conditions for walking and pub garden dining.

J.K. Rowling's Inspirations – Magical Threads in the Cotswolds

- **Why Go:**

  While Rowling has not publicly confirmed exact inspirations, locals often point to Lacock and Gloucester Cathedral as real-world places that strongly influenced the visual tone of Hogwarts and the magical world.

- **Key Locations:**
  - **Lacock Abbey (Wiltshire):** Featured in multiple Harry

75

Potter films — including scenes from Hogwarts corridors and Snape's classroom.

- **Gloucester Cathedral:** Filming site for Hogwarts' cloisters. It's one of the most iconic and recognisable locations from the first two Harry Potter films.

- **Location & Getting There:**

    - Lacock is about 1 hour from Cirencester or Cheltenham by car. Accessible by train to Chippenham, then taxi (approx. £10–£15).

    - Gloucester Cathedral is centrally located in Gloucester, reachable by train from London Paddington in 1.5–2 hours.

- **Costs:**

    - **Lacock Abbey:** Entry via National Trust — £17 adult, free for NT members. (www.nationaltrust.org.uk/lacock)

    - **Gloucester Cathedral:** Entry is free, but a suggested donation of £5 is appreciated. Guided tours cost around £8–£10.

- **Planning Tips:** Arrive early to both locations if visiting in peak season. Lacock can get busy with Potter fans and National Trust members. Combine Gloucester with a visit to Cheltenham or Painswick for a full day out.

Art & Cultural Highlights Nearby

- **Broadway Tower & Arts:**
This 18th-century folly was a gathering point for the Arts & Crafts Movement — William Morris and friends stayed nearby. Broadway village also features small galleries and crafts boutiques. Entry to the tower is £14 (www.broadwaytower.co.uk).

- **Stroud's Art Scene:**
Known for its vibrant creative community, Stroud holds the Stroud Festival of Nature and Site Festival (contemporary art), typically in May–June. Visit the Museum in the Park (free) and browse local artisan markets.

- **Charlbury & Ditchley Park:**
A lesser-known literary connection is Ditchley Park, where Winston Churchill conducted secret wartime meetings. While access is limited, Charlbury's bookshop and pubs retain that classic English literary ambience.

Trip Planning Summary

Location	Key Experience	Cost (2025)	Best Access Point

Location	Attraction	Price	Access
Bampton	Downton Abbey village filming	Free	Car/bus from Oxford
Highclere Castle	Downton manor house	£29–£36	Drive from Oxford/Burford
Slad	Laurie Lee countryside	Free	Taxi from Stroud
Lacock Abbey	Harry Potter filming	£17 (NT entry)	Train + taxi from Chippenham
Gloucester Cathedral	Hogwarts corridors	Donation-based	Train to Gloucester
Broadway Tower	Arts & Crafts site	£14	Drive from Broadway/Moreton-in-Marsh

Final Tips:

- If you're a literature lover, base yourself in Stroud or Cirencester for easy access to Laurie Lee country and day trips to Gloucester and Cheltenham.
- For film and TV buffs, combine Bampton and Lacock into a weekend with an overnight stay in Burford or Chippenham.

- Always check opening times, as some houses (like Highclere or Lacock) have limited seasonal access.

The Cotswolds is a region where stories — both real and imagined — come alive in the landscape, buildings, and people. Whether retracing the steps of famous authors or spotting familiar scenes from the screen, the journey is as rich as the heritage that inspired it.

Family-Friendly Activities

The Cotswolds is a remarkably family-friendly destination, offering a perfect mix of hands-on attractions, educational experiences, and outdoor adventures that can suit toddlers, teens, and adults alike. Whether you're after animals, castles, nature walks, or interactive museums, there's something for every age group. Below is an in-depth guide to family-friendly activities across the region — including costs, locations, and planning tips — based on real experience visiting with children of varying ages.

1. Cotswold Wildlife Park & Gardens – Burford

Why Go:

This is hands down one of the best family attractions in the region. Spread over 160 acres, the park houses over 260 animal species — from lions, rhinos, and giraffes to penguins and lemurs. What sets it apart is the open layout and extensive gardens, making it easy for kids to roam while adults enjoy the landscaping and picnic areas.

Highlights:

- Children's Farmyard with goats, rabbits, and chickens
- Giraffe walkway at eye-level
- Narrow-gauge railway (April–October)
- Large adventure playground and picnic spots

Cost (2025):

- **Adults:** £20
- **Children (3–16):** £13.50
- **Under 3s:** Free
- **Railway ride:** £1.50 per person
  (**Website:** www.cotswold wildlife park.co.uk)

Location & Access:

Located just 2 miles south of Burford, with free parking on site. Buses are limited; best accessed by car.

2. The Cotswold Farm Park – Guiting Power (Adam Henson's Farm)

Why Go:

Run by BBC Countryfile's Adam Henson, this is a working farm that's perfect for young kids and especially great for spring lambing or autumn harvest events. It combines education with fun — kids can bottle-feed lambs, learn about rare breeds, and ride tractors.

Highlights:

- Touch Barn with rabbits and chicks
- Adventure Barn (indoor soft play)
- Tractor Safari Ride
- Outdoor play zones

Cost (2025):

- **Adults:** £17.50
- **Children (4–15):** £16.50
- **Under 4s:** Free
- Online booking recommended for peak times
  (**Website:** www.cotswold farm park.co.uk)

Location & Access:

Near Guiting Power, best reached by car from Stow-on-the-Wold or Bourton-on-the-Water (approx. 15–20 minutes).

3. Birdland Park & Gardens – Bourton-on-the-Water

Why Go:

This smaller-scale park offers a relaxed, shaded experience with exotic birds, penguins, parrots, and a very popular Dinosaur Trail for younger children. It's especially great for under-10s, and it's walkable from the village centre, making it ideal as part of a day in Bourton.

Highlights:

- Penguin Coast (feeding times are fun)
- Dino Dig activity area
- Jurassic Journey life-size dinosaur walk
- Daily talks and feeding sessions

Cost (2025):

- **Adults:** £13.95
- **Children (3–15):** £9.95
- **Under 3s:** Free
  (**Website:** www.birdland.co.uk)

Location & Access:

Centrally located in Bourton-on-the-Water. No parking on-site, but village car parks are nearby (approx. £4 for 4 hours).

4. Model Village & Dragonfly Maze – Bourton-on-the-Water

Why Go:

Two charming experiences side by side. The Model Village is a perfect 1:9 scale replica of Bourton itself, including a miniature version of the model village — a quirky favorite with young children. The Dragonfly Maze combines a hedge maze with a puzzle-solving challenge, perfect for older kids (6+).

Cost (2025):

- **Model Village:** Adults £5, Children £4
- **Dragonfly Maze:** Adults £4.50, Children £4
  (Both are pay-on-entry)

Tip: You can see all of these attractions within walking distance in a single afternoon.

5. Westonbirt Arboretum – Tetbury

Why Go:

One of the UK's finest tree collections, the National Arboretum is incredibly family-friendly, with seasonal trails, Gruffalo-themed walks, and an amazing Treetop Walkway that gives kids a chance to run wild in a safe environment. It's particularly stunning in autumn (for foliage) and spring.

Highlights:

- Treetop Walkway (300m long)
- Family trails and kids' activity packs
- Gruffalo Spotting App (interactive nature trail)

Cost (2025):

- **Adults:** £13
- **Children (5–18):** £4
- **Under 5s:** Free
  (**Website:** www.forestryengland.uk/westonbirt)

Location & Access:

Near Tetbury. Large car park (£2–£3 for parking). No direct public transport; best by car.

6. Gloucester Waterways Museum – Gloucester

Why Go:

Housed in a historic Victorian warehouse at Gloucester Docks, this is an interactive, indoor family stop perfect for rainy days. Kids can learn how locks work, dress as canal boaters, and operate model boats.

Highlights:

- Hands-on exhibits and interactive zones
- Canal boat rides (in summer)
- Excellent café and gift shop

Cost (2025):

- **Adults:** £8
- **Children (5–16):** £5
- **Under 5s:** Free
  (**Website:** www.nwhm.org.uk)

Location & Access:

Walkable from Gloucester Station. Public parking available nearby.

7. Puzzlewood – Forest of Dean

Why Go:

This ancient woodland looks straight out of a fantasy movie — and it has been, featuring in Star Wars, Harry Potter, and Merlin. With moss-covered rocks, winding trails, and secret caves, it's a magical place for imaginative play.

Cost (2025):

- **Adults:** £9
- **Children (3–16):** £8
- **Family (2+2):** £32
  (**Website:** www.puzzlewood.net)

Location & Access:

Near Coleford, around a 1-hour drive from Cirencester. Not suitable for strollers due to uneven terrain.

Practical Tips for Families

- **Transport:** Most attractions are best accessed by car. If you're relying on public transport, base yourself in larger towns like Cheltenham, Cirencester, or Stroud, which have better bus/train connectivity.
- **Dining:** Look for family-friendly pubs like The Plough Inn in Cold Aston or The Bell at Sapperton, both offering children's menus and garden seating.
- **Accommodation:** Many farm stays, such as Notgrove Holidays or Cotswold Farm Park Lodges, offer self-catering cottages with child-friendly facilities like games rooms, animals, and play areas.
- **Booking:** Some attractions (like Cotswold Farm Park or Westonbirt) require online booking during weekends and school holidays. Always check their websites.

The Cotswolds is a region where history, nature, and creativity blend into an ideal playground for families. With careful planning, even a short break can be filled with memorable, enriching experiences — and yes, there's plenty to keep both the kids and adults smiling.

Romantic Getaways & Luxury Retreats In The Cotswolds

The Cotswolds is tailor-made for romantic escapes, with honey-stone cottages, winding country lanes, and luxury hideaways that feel both indulgent and deeply tranquil. Whether it's a long weekend or a honeymoon, this region delivers timeless charm blended with high-end amenities and exceptional service. Having visited numerous times for both romantic retreats and reviews, I can confidently recommend the following experiences and properties.

1. Barnsley House (Near Cirencester)

- **Why Go:** This is a quintessential romantic haven. A 17th-century manor with only 18 rooms, it's known for its award-winning spa and landscaped gardens (designed by the legendary Rosemary Verey). You're tucked away in peaceful countryside yet only 4 miles from Cirencester.
- **Room Rates:** From £350/night, B&B (2025 rate)
- **Highlights:** Private cinema, spa garden retreat, candlelit dining, bicycles for hire
- **Sustainability:** Solar panels, on-site kitchen garden, low-impact amenities

2. The Fish Hotel, Broadway (Farncombe Estate)

- **Why Go:** This woodland-styled retreat offers rustic luxury, perfect for couples who want a mix of outdoorsy charm and pampering. Their treehouses and shepherd's huts with private hot tubs are ideal for a romantic escape.
- **Room Rates:** From £250/night (huts), Treehouses from £390/night
- **Highlights:** Outdoor cinema in summer, forest walks, wine tasting
- **Sustainability:** Solar energy, eco-conscious building design, locally sourced menus
- **Location:** Just outside Broadway, Worcestershire

3. Thyme – Southrop Manor Estate

- **Why Go:** This boutique estate brands itself as a "village within a village," and is an excellent choice for couples who love refined country luxury. There's a cookery school, spa, botanical bar, and peaceful gardens — all very private and stylish.
- **Room Rates:** From £420/night (midweek), with packages available
- **Location:** Southrop, Gloucestershire
- **Sustainability:** Regenerative farming practices, zero-waste kitchens, wildflower meadows

4. Dormy House Hotel & Spa – Broadway

- **Why Go:** Perched above Broadway on the Farncombe Estate, this is a classic Cotswolds country house hotel with ultra-modern spa facilities. Great for spa-focused weekends or "switch-off" retreats.
- **Room Rates:** From £360–£500/night
- **Highlights:** Mud room spa treatments, rooftop hot tub, relaxed luxury

Romantic Things to Do:

- Private hot air balloon rides over the Cotswolds – from £150 per person (seasonal)
- Couples spa treatments at Calcot Spa (Tetbury) or C-Side Spa at Cowley Manor
- Sunset walks in Minchinhampton Common or Broadway Tower
- Private dining at The Wild Rabbit in Kingham – 3-course dinner from £60pp

Sustainable & Eco-friendly Travel In The Cotswolds

Sustainability is increasingly embedded in how the Cotswolds operates — from farm-to-fork dining to off-grid accommodations and rewilding projects. If you want to travel mindfully, there are plenty of ways to experience the region with a lighter footprint, without sacrificing comfort or style.

Eco-Accommodation Options

- **The Cotswold Eco Lodge (Nailsworth):** Solar-powered, low-energy design, rainwater harvesting; self-catering; from £180/night
- **Log House Holidays (Cirencester):** Off-grid wooden cabins on a private lake; no Wi-Fi, 100% solar power; from £250/night
- **Notgrove Holidays (Near Bourton):** Glamping pods, safari tents, and lodges powered by wind and solar; pet-friendly, car-free trails
- **Campwell Woods (Near Bath):** Sustainable woodland cabins and off-grid glamping; communal kitchen; from £140/night

Sustainable Eating & Drinking

- **Daylesford Organic Farm (Near Kingham):** This is a mecca for sustainable dining, offering meals made with ingredients grown metres from your table. Farm tours, zero-waste cooking classes, and organic wine are also on offer. Meals from £15–£25.
- **The Wild Rabbit (Kingham):** Uses local and estate-grown produce. BREEAM-certified renovation. Mains from £20–£35.
- **Stroud Farmers' Market:** One of the best in the UK for organic and ethical produce. Open every Saturday, 9am–2pm.

Sustainable Transport Tips

- **Electric Car Charging:** Most luxury stays now provide EV chargers. Tesla Superchargers are available in Cirencester, Cheltenham, and Burford.
- **Rail Access:** Kingham, Moreton-in-Marsh, and Charlbury have direct services from London Paddington. From there, you can use e-bike rentals (e.g., from Cotswold eBikes, £40/day) or taxis.
- **Walking Routes:** Embrace low-impact travel by walking parts of the Cotswold Way, Windrush Way, or Wardens Way, many of which connect small villages and reduce driving.

Tips for a Romantic & Eco-Friendly Itinerary

- **Plan off-season:** Visit in late spring (May–June) or early autumn (September) for quieter trails and lower carbon impact.
- **Book local:** Choose local-run properties over chains, and ask your hotel about green certifications (Green Tourism, EarthCheck).
- **Slow travel:** Spend longer in one area — for example, base yourself in Broadway or Kingham for 3–4 days and explore on foot, horseback, or by e-bike.

The Cotswolds offers an unparalleled blend of luxury and sustainability. Whether you're toasting in a treehouse hot tub, foraging on an organic farm, or hiking through conservation areas, it's possible to enjoy a deeply rewarding — and responsible — romantic escape in this timeless landscape.

Chapter 5: Curated Itineraries

3-Day Cotswolds Highlights Itinerary

- **Perfect For:** First-timers or short-stay travelers who want to see iconic villages, countryside charm, and experience quintessential Cotswolds elegance.
- **Best Base:** Stow-on-the-Wold or Bourton-on-the-Water (well-connected and centrally located)

Day 1: Northern Cotswolds – Broadway, Chipping Campden & Hidcote

- **Morning:**
  Start at Broadway, often called the "Jewel of the Cotswolds." Stroll the High Street, lined with golden-hued buildings, and stop for breakfast at Broadway Deli (around £12). Climb Broadway Tower (£15 entry) for panoramic views and a romantic hilltop walk.

- **Midday:**
  Drive (15 min) or take a taxi to Chipping Campden, a market town famous for arts & crafts heritage. Visit the Old Silk Mill and Market Hall (free), then lunch at Eight Bells Inn (mains £16–£25).

- **Afternoon:**
  Head to Hidcote Manor Garden (National Trust, £16 entry) for one of England's finest arts and crafts gardens. Nearby Kiftsgate Court Gardens (£10) is another option.

- **Evening:**
  Stay at The Lygon Arms in Broadway (from £240/night) or Noel Arms Hotel in Chipping Campden (from £120/night). Dinner at Russell's of Broadway (3-course menu ~£45pp).

Day 2: Central Cotswolds – Stow, Bourton, Slaughters

- **Morning:**
  Visit Stow-on-the-Wold, browse antiques and local shops, and enjoy breakfast at The Hive (from £10).

- **Midday:**
  Drive (10 min) to Bourton-on-the-Water – stroll by the River Windrush and explore Model Village (£5.95) or Cotswold Motoring Museum (£7.95).

- **Afternoon:**
  Walk or drive to Lower Slaughter (1.5 miles), then follow the Warden's Way to Upper Slaughter – an easy 45-minute scenic walk. Return by foot or taxi.

- **Evening:**
  Dine at The Slaughters Manor House (fine dining, mains from £30). Stay overnight in Bourton-on-the-Water (The Old Manse Hotel, from £110) or Lower Slaughter Manor (from £230).

Day 3: Burford & Bibury

- **Morning:**
  Drive (25 min) to Burford, one of the most picturesque high streets in England. Have breakfast at Huffkins Bakery (£8–£12). Explore local shops and St. John the Baptist Church (free).

- **Midday:**
  Continue to Bibury (20 min drive), famous for Arlington Row. Enjoy riverside walks or visit the trout farm (£6 entry).

- **Lunch:**
  Lunch at The Swan Hotel Bibury (mains £18–£30).

- **Departure Options:**
  Return to Moreton-in-Marsh or Kingham train station (30–40 min drive) for onward travel.

Estimated Budget for 3 Days (Mid-Range):

- **Accommodation:** £300–£600
- **Food:** £120–£180
- **Attractions/Entries:** £40–£60
- **Transport (if renting a car):** £130–£150
  Total: £600–£990 for 2 people

5-Day Slow Travel & Hidden Gems Itinerary

- **Perfect For:** Return travelers, nature lovers, or those wanting to dig deeper into authentic village life, walking trails, and local producers.
- **Best Base:** Mix of bases – start in Winchcombe, continue to Stroud, and finish in Kingham/Bledington.

Day 1: Winchcombe & Sudeley Castle

- **Morning to Afternoon:**
  Explore the village of Winchcombe, then visit Sudeley Castle (home of Katherine Parr; entry £19.50). Hike a segment of the Cotswold Way nearby or stroll the Wardens Way.

- **Evening:**
  Stay at The Lion Inn (from £130/night). Dine in-house or at Wesley House (set menu from £38pp).

Day 2: Painswick & Slad Valley

- **Morning:**
  Drive 35 min south to Painswick, known as the "Queen of the Cotswolds." Visit St. Mary's Church and Rococo Garden (£9.50 entry).

- **Afternoon:**
  Drive or walk to Slad, where Laurie Lee wrote Cider with Rosie. Stop for a pint at The Woolpack Inn with stunning valley views.

- **Evening:**
  Stay in Stroud or nearby Minchinhampton (The Bear of Rodborough – from £120/night). Dinner at Falcon Inn, Painswick (mains ~£25).

Day 3: Nailsworth, Bisley, Minchinhampton

- **Morning to Afternoon:**
  Explore artisan shops in Nailsworth. Then visit the commons in Minchinhampton or enjoy a circular walk around Bisley – hidden, untouristed, and rich in character.

- **Evening:**
  Dinner at Wild Garlic Restaurant in Nailsworth (3-course ~£42). Stay overnight in Nailsworth or move north toward Kingham (45–60 min drive).

Day 4: Kingham, Bledington & Daylesford

- **Morning:**
  Wake up in Kingham or Bledington. Have breakfast at Daylesford Organic Farm (farm breakfast ~£14). Tour the farm shop, spa, and cookery school.

- **Afternoon:**
  Cycle or walk through nearby

countryside – rent bikes at Cotswold eBikes (£40/day). Visit St. Leonard's Church in Bledington, then relax at The Kingham Plough.

- **Evening:**
  Stay at The Wild Rabbit in Kingham (luxury rooms from £280) or The King's Head Inn in Bledington (from £150).

Day 5: Naunton & Guiting Power

- **Morning to Early Afternoon:**
  End your trip by heading toward Naunton and Guiting Power, both quiet, beautiful, and perfect for low-key walking and riverside moments. Lunch at The Hollow Bottom Inn, Naunton (mains £15–£25).

- **Departure:**
  Return to Kingham Station or Moreton-in-Marsh for London train (~1hr40 travel time).

Estimated Budget for 5 Days (Mid-Range):

- **Accommodation:** £600–£1000
- **Food:** £200–£300
- **Attractions/Entries:** £50–£80
- **Transport (Car Hire & Fuel):** £180
  Total: £1050–£1560 for 2 people

Planning Tips:

- Book at least 6–8 weeks in advance for spring/summer travel.
- Trains from London Paddington to Kingham or Moreton-in-Marsh take ~90 minutes.
- Walking boots are recommended for off-road trails.
- Choose one or two bases and radiate outward to avoid overpacking days.

These itineraries balance cultural highlights with lesser-known gems, giving you a genuine taste of the Cotswolds — from postcard villages to peaceful commons only locals know.

7-Day Classic Cotswolds Road Trip Itinerary

- **Perfect for:** First-time visitors who want a full but well-paced journey through the quintessential Cotswold highlights, mixing iconic villages, walking trails, historic sites, and delicious local food.
- **Transport:** Self-drive recommended — car hire from Oxford, London Heathrow, or Moreton-in-Marsh. Expect £250–£350/week for a compact car.
- **Best Time to Go:** Late spring (May–June) or early autumn (September) for mild weather and fewer crowds.

Day 1: Arrival & Northern Gateway — Moreton-in-Marsh & Stow-on-the-Wold

- Arrival via train from London Paddington to Moreton-in-Marsh (~1hr 35 min; ~£35 return).
- Explore Moreton's Tuesday market, traditional pubs, and tea rooms.
- Continue to Stow-on-the-Wold, 10 min drive away. Stroll the market square, visit the famous Yew Tree Door at St. Edward's Church, and browse antique shops.
- **Dinner at:** The Old Stocks Inn (mains £18–£28).
- **Stay:** The Porch House, Stow (from £140/night).

Day 2: Iconic Villages – Bourton-on-the-Water, Lower & Upper Slaughter

- **Morning:** Head to Bourton-on-the-Water, often dubbed "Venice of the Cotswolds." Visit Model Village (£5.95) and Cotswold Motoring Museum (£7.95).
- **Lunch:** Bakery on the Water (from £10).
- **Afternoon:** Walk or drive the scenic 1.5-mile route to Lower Slaughter, then continue to Upper Slaughter. Ideal for gentle riverside walking and peaceful views.
- **Stay:** The Slaughters Manor House (from £240/night).
- **Dinner at:** On-site or Lords of the Manor (tasting menu from £75pp).

Day 3: Broadway & Chipping Campden

- **Morning:** Drive to Broadway (25 min). Climb Broadway Tower (£15) and walk the surrounding deer park.
- **Afternoon:** Head to Chipping Campden, explore the Market Hall, and walk a stretch of the Cotswold Way trail.
- **Stay:** Cotswold House Hotel (from £190/night).
- **Dinner:** Eight Bells Inn (mains £17–£24).

Day 4: Historic Castles & Gardens – Hidcote & Sudeley Castle

- **Morning:** Tour Hidcote Manor Garden (NT, £16), a top example of Arts and Crafts landscaping.
- **Afternoon:** Drive south to Winchcombe and visit Sudeley Castle (£19.50).
- **Stay:** The Lion Inn, Winchcombe (from £130/night).
- **Dinner:** 5 North Street (Michelin-recommended, £40–£55).

Day 5: Cirencester & Bibury

- **Morning:** Head to Cirencester, explore the Corinium Museum (£8.50), and Roman Amphitheatre.
- **Afternoon:** Continue to Bibury – visit Arlington Row, one of the most photographed streets in England.
- **Stay:** The Swan Hotel, Bibury (from £180/night).
- **Dinner:** On-site restaurant (mains £22–£30).

Day 6: Painswick & Stroud

- **Morning:** Drive to Painswick, visit St. Mary's Church and Rococo Garden (£9.50).
- **Afternoon:** Explore Stroud's Saturday Farmers' Market or walk in Slad Valley.
- **Stay:** Court House Manor, Painswick (from £150).
- **Dinner:** The Falcon Inn (mains £18–£25).

Day 7: Burford & Departure

- Final stop in Burford, a gateway to the eastern Cotswolds. Enjoy the high street, Tolsey Museum, and breakfast at Huffkins.
- Return to Oxford or Moreton-in-Marsh for train connections.

Approximate Budget (Per Person):

- **Accommodation (Mid-range):** £900–£1200

- **Food & Drink:** £250–£350
- **Attractions:** £80–£110
- **Car Hire & Fuel:** £150–£200
  Total: £1400–£1800 per person (double occupancy)

10-Day In-Depth Cultural & Scenic Cotswolds Route

Perfect for: Cultural explorers and repeat visitors wanting a deeper dive into the region's literary sites, historic villages, slow travel experiences, and less-crowded gems.

Day 1–2: Charlbury, Witney & Swinbrook

- Explore Wychwood Forest walks, visit Charlbury Museum (free), and enjoy tea at Charlbury Deli & Café.
- Drive to Witney for traditional wool heritage, see Cogges Manor Farm (£7.50).
- Stay at The Swan Inn, Swinbrook (from £130/night).

Day 3–4: Kingham, Daylesford & Bledington

- Explore Daylesford Organic Farm, do a cookery class or spa session (classes from £55).
- Walk or cycle around Kingham and Bledington.
- Stay at The Wild Rabbit (from £250/night).
- Dinner at The Kingham Plough or Bledington's King's Head Inn.

Day 5–6: Tetbury, Nailsworth & Westonbirt Arboretum

- Visit Chavenage House (£10 tours), Highgrove Gardens (pre-booked tours from £30).
- Explore Tetbury's antique shops and Nailsworth's foodie scene.
- Visit Westonbirt Arboretum (£13–£15).
- Stay at The Close Hotel, Tetbury (from £160/night).

Day 7–8: Painswick, Bisley & Laurie Lee's Slad Valley

- Walk the Laurie Lee Wildlife Way, stopping at The Woolpack Inn for a pint and views.
- Discover Bisley, a completely non touristy gem with amazing stone cottages and ancient wells.
- Stay at Tibbiwell Lodge, Painswick (from £110).

Day 9: Berkeley & Dursley

- Visit Berkeley Castle (home of Edward Jenner; £14.50).
- Continue to Dursley, hike Stinchcombe Hill or visit Uley Bury Iron Age Hillfort.
- Stay at The Malt House Hotel, Berkeley (from £100).

Day 10: Cheltenham & Gloucester (Departure)

- Visit Gloucester Cathedral (free entry, donation suggested), explore the Docks and the Waterways Museum (£10).
- Stroll Cheltenham's Montpellier and grab lunch before departing.

Estimated Budget (Per Person):

- **Accommodation (mid-upper range):** £1200–£1600
- **Food & Drink:** £400–£600
- **Attractions:** £120–£150
- **Car Hire & Fuel:** £200–£250
    Total: £1900–£2600 per person (double occupancy)

These curated road trips combine local heritage, beautiful landscapes, and unforgettable village charm. They are crafted from real experience — not just bucket list stops, but real moments of connection and immersion in Cotswolds culture.

Seasonal Itineraries in the Cotswolds:

Spring Blossom & Gardens Itinerary (Late March to Mid-May)

Why Go in Spring:

Spring in the Cotswolds is simply enchanting — it's when the region comes alive with lamb-filled meadows, vibrant wildflowers, blossoming orchards, and some of the finest heritage gardens in England. The crowds are still light compared to summer, accommodation is often 10–20% cheaper, and walking trails are lush and peaceful.

Top Highlights:

Day 1: Painswick & Rococo Garden

- Start in Painswick, known as "The Queen of the Cotswolds."
- **Visit Painswick Rococo Garden (Entry £9.50)** — this hidden gem is one of the best spring garden experiences in the UK, especially for its snowdrops in early spring and later for cherry blossom and heritage fruit trees.
- **Lunch:** Falcon Inn or Cotswold Baguettes.
- Optional 4-mile circular walk into the surrounding countryside.
- **Stay:** Court House Manor (from £140/night).

Day 2: Hidcote Manor Garden & Kiftsgate Court

- Drive to Hidcote Manor Garden (NT, £16.50) near Chipping Campden — spring is prime time for tulips, flowering magnolia, and the first wave of perennials.
- Just across the lane is Kiftsgate Court Gardens (open from April, £10), known for its family-run charm and tiered spring borders.
- **Stay nearby:** Cotswold House Hotel in Chipping Campden (from £180).

Day 3: Abbey House Gardens & Malmesbury

- Explore the market town of Malmesbury, then tour the romantic Abbey House Gardens (£10, seasonal). Known as "The Home of the Naked Gardeners," this private garden is stunning in spring with primroses, hellebores, and emerging roses.
- **Walk:** Along the Avon River by the weir.
- **Stay:** The Old Bell Hotel, Malmesbury (from £160).

Optional Add-on:

- Visit Sezincote House & Gardens (near Moreton-in-Marsh, £15) — a unique Indian-style manor with formal spring gardens and tulip displays.

Spring Travel Tips:

- **Best time:** Late March for snowdrops, April for tulips and cherry blossom, May for bluebells and early roses.

- **What to Pack:** Waterproof walking boots, layered clothing, and a foldable umbrella — spring weather can be unpredictable.

- **Transport:** Best done by car; otherwise, use rail to Moreton-in-Marsh or Stroud and book local taxis (~£15–£25 per journey).

- **Costs:** Expect £130–£200 per night for boutique hotels, meals from £15–£30 per person at local pubs or inns.

Summer Walks & Lavender Fields Itinerary (Late June to Late July)

Why Go in Summer:

Summer in the Cotswolds is peak season for its most iconic landscapes — rolling golden hills, honey-stone villages glowing in sunlight, and striking lavender fields in full bloom. It's ideal for scenic walking, garden visits, and lazy lunches in pub gardens. Do book accommodation early, as July is very popular.

Top Highlights:

Day 1: Snowshill & Cotswold Lavender Farm

- Begin your trip with a visit to Cotswold Lavender Farm near Snowshill (open mid-June to early August; £7.50 entry). The rows of deep-purple lavender against the hills are simply photogenic, and you can buy fresh lavender products onsite.

- **Lunch:** At the on-site tearoom or Snowshill Arms.

- Explore the nearby Snowshill Manor (NT, £14), filled with eccentric collections and surrounded by cottage-style gardens.

- **Stay:** The Broadway Hotel (from £180/night).

Day 2: Bourton-on-the-Hill to Sezincote Walk (6 miles)

- Start in Bourton-on-the-Hill, walk through meadows and wooded paths to the exotic Sezincote House — its Indian-style dome and Mughal gardens are stunning in summer.

- Return loop via the Heart of England Way.

- **Stay nearby:** The Horse & Groom (from £140).

Day 3: Cirencester Park & Riverside Picnic in Bibury

- Morning walk through Cirencester Park, a vast 3,000-acre landscaped estate with open walking trails (free).

- **Afternoon:** Drive to Bibury, enjoy a scenic riverside picnic by Rack Isle (shop for treats at Jesse Smith Farm Shop beforehand).

- Optional stop at Arlington Row for iconic photos.

- **Stay:** The Swan Hotel in Bibury (from £170).

Day 4: Slad Valley & Literary Landscape Walk (4–5 miles)

- Begin at The Woolpack Inn, walk the circular route through Slad Valley, following the footsteps of poet Laurie Lee (author of Cider with Rosie).
- Gorgeous wildflower-strewn meadows and Cotswold stone hamlets.
- **Lunch:** Return to the Woolpack.
- **Stay nearby:** Painswick's The Falcon or Tibbiwell Lodge.

Summer Travel Tips:

- **Best time:** Late June–late July for lavender, roses, and wildflower meadows.
- **Book Early:** Lavender fields are very popular — visit early in the morning or after 4 PM to avoid crowds.
- **Stay Cool:** Many hotels don't have A/C — check before booking.
- **Walking Gear:** Lightweight walking shoes, sunscreen, hat, and water bottle essential.

Costs Summary (Per Person for 3–4 Days):

- **Accommodation:** £450–£750
- **Food & Drink:** £100–£200
- **Entry Fees & Attractions:** £30–£60
- **Transport (Car Hire or Rail + Local Taxi):** £150–£200

Both itineraries offer an immersive way to experience the Cotswolds through its changing seasons. Spring is gentler, more floral and quiet, while summer is vibrant, photogenic, and alive with colour and energy. Choose based on your pace — or better still, plan to return and enjoy both.

Seasonal Itineraries: Autumn Foliage & Harvest Festivals

(Late September to Early November)

Why Go in Autumn:

Autumn in the Cotswolds is a sensory feast — a time when golden light bathes the honey-hued stone villages, woodlands burst into reds and ambers, and farm shops overflow with apples, squash, and pumpkins. It's quieter than summer, accommodation rates drop by 15–20%, and seasonal events like apple pressing, harvest suppers, and food festivals make it ideal for those who love nature and local culture.

Top Places for Autumn Colour:

- **Westonbirt Arboretum (Nr Tetbury, Entry £13–£15):** One of the UK's best places for autumn colour with over 15,000 trees. Visit in mid-October for peak Japanese maple foliage.
- **Batsford Arboretum (Moreton-in-Marsh, Entry £9.95):** Excellent for acers, oaks, and rare tree species. Don't miss the café overlooking the autumnal landscape.
- **Slad Valley & Laurie Lee Wildlife Way:** A 5-mile circular route through meadows, beech woods, and historic hamlets — absolutely glowing in late October.

Seasonal Food Experiences:

- **Harvest Suppers & Apple Days:** Check local pubs and village halls in October for events like:
  - **Daylesford Organic Apple Day (Mid-Oct, near Kingham):** Family-friendly with cider tasting, orchard tours, and harvest foods.

- **Stroud Apple Day (Oct, FREE):** A lively community festival with heritage apples, fresh-pressed juice, and local food stalls.

- **Farm Shops to Visit:**
  - **The Cotswold Farm Park (Adams Farm):** Pumpkin picking from mid-Oct; Entry £12.50
  - **Burford Garden Company's Autumn Food Fair (Late Sept):** Free entry; excellent for artisan cheese, preserves, and kitchenware.

Where to Stay:

- **The Rectory Hotel (Crudwell):** A classic countryside autumn retreat with fireside dining (from £170/night).
- **The Painswick (Painswick):** Stylish, quiet, and surrounded by wooded valleys (£160–£250/night).

Planning Tips:

- **Best time:** October 10–25 for peak foliage.
- **Getting around:** A car is ideal for accessing the arboretums and rural festivals.
- **Packing:** Bring a waterproof coat, walking boots, and layers — mornings and evenings are crisp.

Winter Getaways & Cozy Villages

(December through February)

Why Go in Winter:

Winter in the Cotswolds is deeply atmospheric — think frosty mornings, log fires in stone pubs, twinkling villages with tasteful Christmas lights, and peaceful walking trails. If you're looking for a romantic escape, a quiet writers' retreat, or a festive break, this is the best time to enjoy the region without crowds.

Top Experiences:

1. Christmas Markets & Illuminations

- **Cirencester Christmas Market & Lights Switch-On (Late Nov–Dec):** One of the most festive in the region, with real reindeer, mulled wine, and local crafts.
- **Broadway Late Night Shopping & Market (1st & 2nd Fridays of Dec):** Atmospheric evening with roasted chestnuts and fairy-lit windows. FREE entry.
- **Sudeley Castle's Spectacle of Light (Mid Nov–Dec; Entry £19.50):** A magical illuminated trail through the gardens and ruins, suitable for all ages.

2. Cozy Villages & Romantic Pubs

- **Snowshill & Stanton:** Beautiful in snow or frost, these two small villages are almost untouched in winter — perfect for photo stops and peaceful walks.
- **Lower Slaughter Manor or The Slaughters Inn:** Ideal for a romantic dinner by the fireplace (rooms from £160–£220; meals from £25–£40 per person).

3. Countryside Walks

- **Cleeve Hill Circular Walk:** Breathtaking views even in frosty conditions. Layer up!
- **Bourton-on-the-Water's Christmas Tree in the River:** An iconic festive sight, best seen at dusk in December.

Where to Stay:

- **Dormy House (Broadway):** Spa, roaring fires, luxury winter packages (from £250/night in low season).
- **The Wild Rabbit (Kingham):** Michelin-rated pub with boutique rooms and seasonal game dishes (£200–£350/night).

Winter Travel Tips:

- **Accommodation:** Many properties offer 2–3 night winter break deals from January to early March.
- **Packing:** Warm, waterproof gear is essential — icy days are common.
- **Driving:** Roads are gritted, but narrow lanes can be slick — rent a small 4WD if planning to explore remote spots.

Costs Summary (Per Person for 3 Days):

- **Accommodation:** £350–£600
- **Food & Drink:** £90–£180
- **Festive Event Entry:** £10–£25 per activity
- **Transport:** Car hire (£100–£150 for 3 days); rail/taxi combo slightly more

Final Thoughts:

Autumn and winter in the Cotswolds are for those seeking atmosphere, comfort, and authenticity. Whether you're sipping cider at a harvest festival or curling up with a book by a pub fire in Bibury, these seasons reveal a quieter, deeper charm of the region — one that's often missed by summer visitors. You'll return home rested, well-fed, and likely already planning your next off-season trip.

Chapter 6 : Practical Tips & Resources

Packing Guide for All Seasons

Packing smartly for the Cotswolds is essential to fully enjoy your trip, as the region's weather can be variable and activities diverse. Whether you're visiting in spring, summer, autumn, or winter, here's what to bring for each season and some universal essentials.

Spring (March – May):

- **Weather:** Mild but unpredictable, temperatures range from 8°C to 16°C, occasional showers.
- **Clothing:**
    - Waterproof jacket or trench coat
    - Layered clothing: light sweaters, long-sleeve shirts, T-shirts
    - Comfortable walking shoes or waterproof boots (many trails can be muddy)
    - Light scarf and hat for cooler mornings
- **Other essentials:** Umbrella, sunglasses, insect repellent (for woodland walks), reusable water bottle

Summer (June – August):

- **Weather:** Generally warm and pleasant, 18°C to 25°C, but rain showers possible.
- **Clothing:**
    - Lightweight tops and shorts/trousers
    - Sunhat and sunglasses
    - Light raincoat or compact umbrella
    - Good walking shoes or trainers (many villages have cobblestones)
    - Swimwear (if you plan to visit local lidos or hotel pools)
- **Other essentials:** Sunscreen (the Cotswolds are quite rural, so sunburn can sneak up), insect repellent

Autumn (September – November):

- **Weather:** Cooling down, 10°C to 17°C, often wet and windy.
- **Clothing:**
    - Warm layers: sweaters, fleeces
    - Waterproof jacket and sturdy walking boots (preferably waterproof)
    - Gloves and hat for late autumn
    - Comfortable clothes for indoor dining or pubs
- **Other essentials:** Backpack for day hikes, reusable water bottle, camera (for spectacular autumn colours)

Winter (December – February):

- **Weather:** Cold, 0°C to 8°C, often damp with frost or occasional snow.
- **Clothing:**
    - Thermal base layers (especially if walking outdoors)
    - Heavy waterproof coat or insulated jacket
    - Warm hat, scarf, gloves
    - Waterproof, insulated boots with good grip for icy paths
    - Smart casual clothes for cozy pubs or luxury retreats

- **Other essentials:** Lip balm, moisturizer, portable phone charger, torch/flashlight if walking after dark

Universal Essentials (All Seasons):

- **Daypack:** For carrying water, snacks, maps, and layers.
- **Travel adapter:** UK plug if coming from abroad.
- **Map or GPS app:** The Cotswolds have spotty mobile reception in rural areas; paper maps or offline GPS apps (like OS Maps) are useful.
- **Cash and cards:** Most places accept cards but some smaller shops and farm markets prefer cash.
- **Medication and personal hygiene:** Carry basics and any prescriptions.

Accessibility Information

The Cotswolds is a largely rural area with many historic villages, uneven pavements, and narrow lanes. However, there have been significant improvements to make the region more accessible for visitors with mobility issues, sensory impairments, or other disabilities.

General Accessibility Overview:

- **Transport:**
  - Major towns like Cheltenham, Cirencester, and Stroud have accessible buses and taxis.
  - Car hire companies offer vehicles with hand controls upon request; driving yourself is often the best way to reach rural spots.
  - Train stations at Moreton-in-Marsh, Kemble, and Kingham have step-free access and staff assistance available (advance notice recommended).

- **Walking Trails:**
  - The Cotswold Way National Trail offers some sections that are wheelchair accessible or suitable for mobility scooters, especially near towns such as Chipping Campden and Winchcombe. However, many trails are hilly and uneven.
  - Local circular walks vary in difficulty; check the Cotswolds National Landscape website or local tourist offices for graded walks.
  - Some village centers have cobblestones and narrow footpaths — bring suitable mobility aids and plan accordingly.

Accessible Attractions:

- **Hidcote Manor Garden:** Provides mobility scooter hire (£10 per day) and wheelchair access on most paths. Toilets and parking are wheelchair accessible.
- **Blenheim Palace:** Extensive step-free access, accessible parking, and wheelchair-friendly shuttle buses around the grounds.
- **Sudeley Castle:** Wheelchair accessible in most areas; accessible toilets and parking available.
- **Cotswold Wildlife Park:** Offers accessible paths and wheelchair hire on site.
- **Museum of Cotswold Life (Cirencester):** Fully accessible with

step-free entrances and accessible toilets.

Accessible Accommodation:

Many hotels and B&Bs in the Cotswolds now provide accessible rooms with wet rooms, ramps, and wider doorways. Examples include:

- **Calcot Manor (near Tetbury):** Luxury hotel with accessible rooms, pool hoists, and accessible spa facilities.
- **The Lygon Arms (Broadway):** Has several accessible rooms and is experienced in accommodating guests with disabilities.
- **Local cottages:** Some holiday cottages have been adapted for wheelchair users; websites like Sykes Cottages or Cotswold Cottages allow filtering for accessibility features.

Tips for Planning:

- **Notify in advance:** Contact accommodation and transport providers to confirm accessibility facilities.
- **Tourist Information Centres:** Cirencester, Cheltenham, and Stow-on-the-Wold TICs have accessibility guides and can help arrange assistance.
- **Medical facilities:** The Cotswolds have well-equipped clinics and hospitals in larger towns; however, rural GP surgeries may have limited hours.

Summary

When packing for the Cotswolds, plan layers and waterproofs for unpredictable weather and terrain, adapting for the season. For accessibility, while some rural areas are challenging, many attractions, accommodations, and transport options are improving. Advance planning and local guidance ensure that all visitors can enjoy the quintessential English countryside experience safely and comfortably.

Traveling with Pets in the Cotswolds

The Cotswolds is an excellent destination for pet owners, especially dog lovers, offering miles of scenic countryside, charming villages, and pet-friendly accommodation and eateries. However, traveling with pets requires some practical planning to ensure a smooth and enjoyable trip for everyone.

Why Bring Your Pet?

The Cotswolds' wide-open spaces, gentle walking trails, and welcoming atmosphere make it a haven for pets, particularly dogs. Many pubs and cafes welcome dogs inside or on patios, and there are numerous off-leash walking spots and dog-friendly attractions.

Pet-Friendly Accommodation:

- Many cottages, B&Bs, and hotels across the Cotswolds openly welcome pets, often charging a modest additional fee (£10–£25 per night).

- Popular pet-friendly places include The Old Stocks Inn in Stow-on-the-Wold, The Wheatsheaf Inn in Northleach, and many self-catering cottages listed on platforms like Sykes Cottages or Airbnb with pet filters.

- Always check the pet policy upfront, including rules about off-leash access, fencing, and local wildlife.

Travel Tips:

- **Transport:** If traveling by car (the most flexible option), bring a secure pet carrier or dog seat belt harness. Keep water, a bowl, and snacks handy for breaks.

- **Public Transport:** Some local buses allow small pets in carriers; check individual policies. Trains may allow dogs, usually free or for a small fee (under 20 pounds).

- **Walking & Outdoor Etiquette:** Many Cotswold trails are dog-friendly, but owners must keep dogs under control, especially near livestock. Some areas, especially farmland and nature reserves, may have seasonal restrictions (check signs).

- **Local Vet Information:** Familiarize yourself with the nearest vets in towns like Cirencester, Cheltenham, or Stow-on-the-Wold, just in case.

Costs to Consider:

- Pet fees for accommodation (£10–£25/night).
- Additional cleaning fees may apply in some places.
- Public transport fees if applicable.
- Food and supplies, including local dog-friendly stores for any forgotten items.

Recommended Pet-Friendly Activities:

- Walking the Cotswold Way sections around Chipping Campden or Broadway—lots of green space.
- Visiting Cotswold Wildlife Park (check pet policy, often dogs allowed on leads in outside areas).
- Exploring village centers like Burford and Bibury where many pubs and shops are pet-friendly.

Photography Tips & Best Viewpoints in the Cotswolds

The Cotswolds' quintessential English charm—with honey-hued limestone cottages, rolling hills, and ancient woodlands—makes it a paradise for photographers. Whether you're a casual snapper or serious enthusiast, capturing the beauty of the region requires some insider tips and knowledge of the best vantage points.

When to Shoot:

- **Golden Hour:** Early morning and late afternoon offer the softest, warmest natural light that enhances the iconic honey stone colors and casts long, dramatic shadows. Sunrise over villages like Castle Combe or Bibury can be magical.

- **Seasonal Variations:**

    - **Spring:** Blossoming gardens, vibrant green fields, and lambs in pastures.
    - **Summer:** Lush landscapes and blue skies, ideal for wide countryside panoramas.
    - **Autumn:** Fiery foliage and harvest scenes, especially around Painswick and Minchinhampton.
    - **Winter:** Crisp frosts, moody skies, and cozy village scenes with smoke curling from chimneys.

Best Viewpoints & Locations:

- **Broadway Tower:** Standing atop the second-highest point in the Cotswolds, this folly offers sweeping panoramic views over 16 counties on clear days—perfect for wide-angle landscape shots.

- **Sudeley Castle Gardens:** Beautifully manicured grounds with historic architecture framed by seasonal blooms.
- **Bourton-on-the-Water:** Capture the charming low bridges over the gentle River Windrush, especially from Mill Bridge or near the Model Village.
- **The Rollright Stones:** Ancient stone circle with atmospheric moorland views—great for mystical dawn shots.
- **Painswick Rococo Gardens:** A unique blend of historic landscaping with quirky features and colorful planting.
- **Lea & Cleverton Hills:** For rugged countryside shots with dramatic skies and classic Cotswold farmland.

Photography Gear & Tips:

- Bring a wide-angle lens for landscapes and village streetscapes, and a telephoto lens for wildlife or distant details.
- Use a tripod for early morning or twilight shots to avoid blur in low light.
- A polarizing filter helps reduce glare and enhances sky contrast.
- Drone photography is popular but check local restrictions—some areas around historic sites may prohibit drones.
- Consider macro lenses for close-ups of flowers, textures of stone walls, or wildlife like butterflies.
- Pack extra batteries and memory cards, as you'll likely shoot extensively.

Practical Advice:

- Plan your day around light conditions; for example, shoot villages from east-facing hills in the morning, then switch to west-facing spots later.
- Be respectful of private property—many Cotswold cottages are lived-in homes. Stick to public footpaths.
- Use local tourist offices or photo guidebooks for lesser-known viewpoints.
- Early weekdays and off-peak seasons (late autumn, winter) offer fewer crowds and unobstructed shots.

Summary

Traveling with pets in the Cotswolds is highly rewarding but requires preparation—from booking pet-friendly accommodation to understanding walking and transport rules. Meanwhile, the region's photogenic beauty, enhanced by ideal lighting and varied vantage points, invites photographers to capture timeless rural England. By planning timing, locations, and equipment wisely, you can create stunning images and memorable experiences in this quintessential English landscape.

Emergency Contacts & Healthcare in the Cotswolds

Emergency Services (Police, Fire, Ambulance):

- **Phone:** 999 (UK-wide emergency number)
- Use this number for any urgent emergencies requiring police, fire, or medical assistance.

Non-Emergency Police Contact:

- **Gloucestershire Police:**
  - **Phone:** 101

- o **Website:** https://www.gloucestershire.police.uk
- o Useful for reporting non-urgent crimes or seeking local advice.

Local Hospitals with A&E (Accident & Emergency):

- **Cheltenham General Hospital**
  - o **Address:** Sandford Road, Cheltenham, GL53 7AN
  - o **Phone:** +44 1242 548000
  - o **About:** Main hospital serving the Cotswolds area with full emergency department.

- **Cirencester Hospital (Minor Injuries Unit)**
  - o **Address:** Tetbury Road, Cirencester, GL7 1YG
  - o **Phone:** +44 1285 654611
  - o **About:** Minor injuries and urgent care (no full A&E).

- **Stroud General Hospital (Minor Injuries Unit)**
  - o **Address:** Trinity Road, Stroud, GL5 2QG
  - o **Phone:** +44 1453 754400
  - o **About:** Minor injuries unit; for more serious emergencies, go to Cheltenham General.

NHS 111 – Non-Emergency Medical Advice:

- **Phone:** 111
- Available 24/7 for urgent but non-life-threatening medical concerns, health advice, and direction to appropriate services.

Pharmacies (Chemists):

- Most towns have local pharmacies open during business hours.
- Larger chains include Boots and Lloyds Pharmacy with extended hours.
- Some offer 24-hour service; check local listings or NHS websites.

Travel Insurance Tip:

- Always have comprehensive travel insurance covering medical emergencies, hospital stays, and possible repatriation.

Planning Tips:

- Save emergency numbers on your phone before arrival.
- Note the nearest hospital or urgent care center based on your accommodation location.
- Know the location of the nearest pharmacy for any medication needs.
- If driving, keep a printed list of emergency contacts in the vehicle.

Local Tour Operators & Experiences in the Cotswolds

1. Cotswold Walks & Cycling Tours – Cotswold Guided Walks

- **Why Go:** The Cotswolds is a walker's paradise with miles of scenic trails. Cotswold Guided Walks offers expertly led walking and cycling tours that reveal hidden gems beyond the typical tourist paths. Their guides are passionate locals who share deep historical knowledge, anecdotes, and insider tips.

- **Experience:** Choose from gentle countryside walks, historic village explorations, or challenging hikes like sections of the Cotswold Way. They also run cycling tours that cater to all levels, with bike hire options included.

- **Cost:** Guided walks start around £25 per person for a half-day tour; full-day tours cost about £50–£60. Cycling tours are around £60–£90 including bike hire.

- **Location:** Tours typically start in popular hubs like Chipping Campden, Moreton-in-Marsh, or Bourton-on-the-Water. Booking is recommended in advance via their website: https://www.cotswoldguidedwalks.co.uk

2. Cotswold Chauffeur Drives & Private Tours

- **Why Go:** For those wanting a luxurious, stress-free way to explore multiple villages and landmarks, private chauffeur tours provide a personalized, comfortable experience with the flexibility to customize your itinerary. Ideal for couples, families, or small groups.

- **Experience:** Visit iconic sites like Sudeley Castle, Hidcote Manor, and quaint villages such as Broadway and Stow-on-the-Wold, all while enjoying expert commentary from your driver-guide. Some tours focus on specific themes like gardens, history, or foodie trails.

- **Cost:** Prices typically start at £300 for a half-day (4 hours), with full-day tours (8 hours) around £550–£600 depending on group size and distance.

- **Booking & Location:** Based in central hubs such as Cheltenham or Cirencester. Many operators take online bookings; search for "Cotswold Chauffeur Tours."

3. Cotswold Farm & Food Tours – The Cotswold Foodie Experience

- **Why Go:** The Cotswolds is famed for its farm-to-table produce, artisan cheese, and traditional ales. Food tours provide a delicious way to discover local flavors, meet producers, and visit historic market towns.

- **Experience:** Tours include visits to local farms, cheese dairies (like the renowned Stow-on-the-Wold Cheese Shop), craft breweries, and quaint tearooms. Sampling sessions and behind-the-scenes access are highlights.

- **Cost:** Half-day food tours run about £65–£80 per person, full-day tours around £120. Some include lunch or afternoon tea.

- **Location:** Common starting points include Moreton-in-Marsh or Cirencester. Book through operators such as Taste Cotswolds or Cotswold Food Tours.

4. Heritage & Castle Tours – Guided Visits to Sudeley Castle, Blenheim Palace & Hidcote Manor

- **Why Go:** To fully appreciate the grandeur and history of these estates, guided tours offer in-depth context that you won't get from audio guides or self-exploration alone. Local guides often add fascinating stories of the aristocracy, architectural details, and gardens.

- **Experience:** Many operators offer half-day or full-day tours combining multiple estates with transport included. Some specialize in history-focused experiences, such as Tudor or Victorian eras.

- **Cost:** Guided estate tours typically range from £45 to £90 per person, depending on inclusions and transport. Admission tickets for these sites range from £15 to £30 if booked separately.

- **Location:** Tours usually depart from major towns like Cheltenham, Cirencester, or Oxford. Check websites of operators like Cotswold Tours & Walks or private heritage tour companies.

5. Photography & Nature Tours

- **Why Go:** The Cotswolds' rolling hills, honey-colored stone cottages, and seasonal colors are a dream for photographers and nature lovers. Specialized tours offer guidance on the best spots, lighting, and composition.

- **Experience:** Join local photographers who lead small groups to iconic viewpoints like Broadway Tower or the villages of Lower Slaughter and Naunton at optimal times for sunrise or sunset. Birdwatching and wildlife spotting tours are also available.

- **Cost:** Typically £50–£75 for half-day group tours; private sessions vary from £150 upwards.

- **Location:** Based around central and northern Cotswolds. Book directly through photography tour providers or nature centres.

How to Plan & Book

- **When to Book:** The Cotswolds sees peak visitor numbers in spring and summer; book popular tours at least 2–4 weeks in advance, especially for weekends or holidays. Winter tours are less frequent but offer unique, quieter experiences.

- **How to Book:** Most operators have user-friendly websites with online booking and clear cancellation policies. Check reviews on TripAdvisor or Google for up-to-date traveler feedback.

- **Transport Tip:** Many tours include transport from town centers, but if not, it's practical to rent a car or use local taxis, as public transport options are limited between villages.

- **Cost Management:** Combine tours or choose half-day options to stay within budget while seeing highlights.

Final Thought

Local tour operators in the Cotswolds are invaluable for gaining deeper insights into this picturesque region's history, culture, and countryside. Whether you're a casual visitor or a serious explorer, joining a well-reviewed local experience will enrich your trip, save you planning time, and ensure you see the best-hidden corners and stories the Cotswolds has to offer.

Cotswolds Souvenirs & What to Bring Home

1. Cotswold Honey & Artisan Jams

- **Why It's Special:** The Cotswolds is known for its wildflower meadows that produce distinctive, fragrant honey. Many local farms and market stalls offer jars of pure Cotswold honey, often accompanied by artisan jams made from seasonal fruits like damsons or raspberries. These edible souvenirs are perfect for food lovers and easy to pack.

- **Where to Buy:**
  - **Cotswold Honey Company** – Available at farm shops like Daylesford Organic Farm Shop (Kingham) or local farmers' markets.
  - **Cost:** £5–£10 per jar depending on size and specialty (e.g., infused varieties).

- **Tip:** Pair with locally baked oatcakes or artisan bread for a true Cotswold breakfast gift.

2. Handcrafted Soaps & Natural Skincare

- **Why It's Special:** The Cotswolds has many small producers crafting soaps, bath salts, and skincare products using natural, locally sourced ingredients like lavender, honey, and herbs. These are ideal for pampering gifts that evoke the countryside.

- **Where to Buy:**
  - The Cotswold Soap Company (based in Stow-on-the-Wold) has beautiful gift sets and single bars available in tearooms and artisan shops.
  - **Cost:** Around £4–£12 per soap bar or small gift sets.

- **Tip:** Look for seasonal scents like lavender in summer or rosemary in winter.

3. Cotswold Wool & Knitwear

- **Why It's Special:** Wool production has a long history here, and quality knitwear or woolen scarves from local producers make authentic, long-lasting souvenirs. Whether a classic scarf or hand-knit gloves, these are practical and stylish reminders of the region.

- **Where to Buy:**
  - The Cotswold Woollen Weavers shop in Chipping Campden offers locally sourced wool products and handmade garments.
  - **Cost:** Scarves and hats typically range from £30 to £80 depending on craftsmanship and material.

- **Tip:** Visit their workshop to see the spinning and weaving process in action.

4. Cotswold Cheese & Local Delicacies

- **Why It's Special:** Artisan cheeses, especially from small dairies, are a must-bring item for food enthusiasts. The region produces award-winning varieties such as Stinking Bishop and Single Gloucester. Pairing cheese with locally made chutneys or crackers makes an excellent gift.

- **Where to Buy:**
  - The Cotswold Cheese Company (Stow-on-the-Wold) or market stalls in Moreton-in-Marsh.
  - **Cost:** Cheese wheels or portions range from £5 for small samples

to £20+ for larger pieces or specialty aged cheeses.

- **Tip:** Check customs regulations if traveling internationally, as dairy products may have restrictions.

---

5. Traditional Pottery & Ceramics

- **Why It's Special:** The Cotswolds has a heritage of pottery making, especially in towns like Stow-on-the-Wold and Chipping Campden. Hand-painted mugs, plates, or decorative pieces featuring classic English countryside motifs make unique souvenirs.

- **Where to Buy:**
    - Potteries such as Cotswold Ceramics (Stow-on-the-Wold) or independent artisan shops.
    - **Cost:** Small items like mugs or bowls range from £15 to £40; larger or more intricate pieces can cost £50+.

- **Tip:** Many shops offer gift wrapping and can ship internationally.

---

6. Books & Local Guides

- **Why It's Special:** For literary lovers, books about the Cotswolds—whether history, nature, or local authors—offer a meaningful keepsake. Titles related to Laurie Lee's Cider with Rosie or guides to local walks deepen your connection to the area.

- **Where to Buy:**
    - Waterstones in Cirencester or independent bookshops in towns like Tetbury and Chipping Campden.
    - **Cost:** Typically £10–£25 per book.

- **Tip:** Pick up a detailed walking guide or a collection of local poetry for a personal touch.

---

7. Handmade Chocolates & Confectionery

- **Why It's Special:** Artisanal chocolate makers and sweet shops in the region produce quality truffles, fudge, and traditional English sweets that are a delicious gift for friends or family.

- **Where to Buy:**
    - The Chocolate Tree (Cirencester) or Fudge Kitchen stalls in various market towns.
    - **Cost:** Boxes or packs from £5 up to £20 for deluxe assortments.

- **Tip:** Visit during market days for special seasonal flavors.

Planning Your Souvenir Shopping

- **Best Places to Shop:**
    - **Market Towns:** Stow-on-the-Wold, Chipping Campden, Moreton-in-Marsh, and Cirencester have the highest concentration of artisan shops and market stalls.
    - **Farm Shops:** Daylesford Organic, Holt Farm, and similar outlets offer a range of local

produce and gifts.

- **Market Days:** Coordinate your visit with local market days (usually Thursdays or Saturdays) for the best variety of handmade goods and fresh produce. For example, Moreton-in-Marsh hosts a popular market every Thursday.

- **Budget:** A modest souvenir shopping budget of around £20–£50 allows you to pick up a combination of food items, small crafts, and keepsakes without overspending.

Summary

The best souvenirs from the Cotswolds reflect the region's natural beauty, traditional crafts, and culinary heritage. From sweet jars of honey and artisan cheeses to wool scarves and handcrafted soaps, there's something authentic and meaningful for every traveler. Shopping locally not only supports the community but ensures you bring home quality products that tell the story of this iconic English region.

Appendices

Glossary of Local Terms & Phrases in the Cotswolds

1. Cotswold Stone

- **Meaning:** The warm, honey-colored limestone unique to the region, used extensively in buildings and walls.
- **Usage:** "Look at that beautiful house made from Cotswold stone — it really captures the area's charm."

2. Village Green

- **Meaning:** The central grassy area in many villages, often used for community events, fairs, or simply as a communal space.
- **Usage:** "The village fete is held every summer on the green."

3. Pub

- **Meaning:** Short for "public house," a traditional English bar and social hub where locals gather for drinks and food.
- **Usage:** "Let's stop by the pub for a pint of local ale."

4. Ale

- **Meaning:** A type of beer, often traditionally brewed and served in pubs. The Cotswolds are known for local craft ales.
- **Usage:** "Try the local ale — it's brewed right here in the Cotswolds."

5. Tearoom

- **Meaning:** A café serving tea, cakes, and light meals, often in a quaint setting. A staple in Cotswold villages.
- **Usage:** "We had a lovely cream tea at the tearoom in Bourton-on-the-Water."

6. Cream Tea

- **Meaning:** A traditional afternoon snack of scones served with clotted cream and strawberry jam, accompanied by tea.
- **Usage:** "Don't miss having a cream tea while you're here — it's quintessentially English."

7. Clotted Cream

- **Meaning:** A thick, rich cream made by heating full-fat cow's milk, commonly served with scones.
- **Usage:** "Spread the clotted cream generously on your scone before the jam."

8. Market Town

- **Meaning:** A small town with a historic right to host markets, often bustling with local vendors on market days.
- **Usage:** "Moreton-in-Marsh is a popular market town with a busy Thursday market."

9. Thatched Roof

- **Meaning:** A traditional roofing method using dry vegetation such as straw or reeds, common in historic cottages.
- **Usage:** "The cottage down the lane has a charming thatched roof."

10. Manor House

- **Meaning:** A large historic country house that was once the center of an estate. Often open to the public.
- **Usage:** "We toured Hidcote Manor House and its stunning gardens."

11. Fete / Village Fete

- **Meaning:** A local fair or festival, often held outdoors with stalls, games, and community activities.
- **Usage:** "The annual village fete is great fun, with homemade cakes and local crafts."

12. Cotswold Lion

- **Meaning:** The nickname for the large, muscular sheep native to the Cotswolds, historically important to the wool trade.
- **Usage:** "You'll see the iconic Cotswold lions grazing in the fields."

13. Footpath / Public Right of Way

- **Meaning:** A path legally open for public walking, often through fields and countryside.
- **Usage:** "The footpath from the village leads straight to the old church."

14. Green Belt

- **Meaning:** Protected countryside areas around towns to prevent urban sprawl, preserving natural beauty.
- **Usage:** "The Cotswolds Green Belt keeps the villages surrounded by open fields."

15. Circular Walk

- **Meaning:** A walking route that starts and ends in the same place, popular for day hikes.
- **Usage:** "We did a lovely circular walk around Lower Slaughter."

16. Farm Shop

- **Meaning:** A retail outlet selling fresh, local produce directly from farms, including meats, cheeses, and baked goods.
- **Usage:** "Pick up some fresh bread and cheese at the farm shop on the way."

17. Alehouse / Inn

- **Meaning:** Historic terms for pubs, especially those offering lodging as well as food and drink.
- **Usage:** "The village inn has been welcoming travelers for centuries."

18. Local Ales / Real Ale

- **Meaning:** Beers brewed locally using traditional methods, often unpasteurized and served from casks.
- **Usage:** "Sample some real ale at the Kings Head pub — it's brewed just down the road."

19. Country Fair

- **Meaning:** A festive event showcasing rural crafts, animals, and local produce, often seasonal.
- **Usage:** "We attended the autumn country fair and bought homemade preserves."

20. Yew Tree

- **Meaning:** A traditional ancient tree often found in churchyards, symbolic in English history and culture.
- **Usage:** "The churchyard is famous for its ancient yew tree."

Basic Phrases & Polite Expressions

- "**Good morning/afternoon**" – Standard greeting, especially polite when entering shops or pubs.
- "**Please**" / "**Thank you**" – Essential politeness in all interactions.
- "**Could I have cream tea, please?**" – Ordering a classic snack politely.
- "**Is this the right way to…?**" – Useful when asking for directions to a village or attraction.
- "**Do you have any local produce?**" – Asking in shops or markets about regional specialties.
- "**What time does the market open?**" – Practical when planning visits.
- "**Is there parking nearby?**" – Helpful for those driving between villages.

- **"Do you recommend any local walks?"** – Great for getting insider tips from locals.
- **"Could you tell me about this cheese/honey?"** – Engaging with producers or sellers at markets.
- **"Where is the nearest pub/tearoom?"** – For social stops and refreshment breaks.
- **"Are dogs allowed here?"** – Useful when traveling with pets, as many places have restrictions.

How This Helps Your Visit

Understanding these local terms and phrases enriches your experience, making interactions smoother and your appreciation of the Cotswolds deeper. Locals take pride in their heritage, and demonstrating knowledge and politeness opens doors to friendlier service and insider recommendations.

Annual Events Calendar 2025–2026
Cotswolds Highlights

The Cotswolds, with its charming villages and historic market towns, hosts a rich array of events throughout the year. These festivals showcase local culture, crafts, food, and seasonal beauty, perfect for visitors aiming to time their trip around memorable experiences.

Spring 2025

- **Cheltenham Literature Festival**
    - **When:** October 4–13, 2025 (late autumn, but worth noting)
    - **Where:** Cheltenham, Gloucestershire
    - **Why Go:** One of the oldest and most prestigious literary festivals in the UK, attracting world-class authors and thinkers. Great for literary lovers wanting talks, workshops, and book signings.
    - **Tickets:** From £10 for individual events, with multi-event passes available. Advance booking recommended.

- **Moreton-in-Marsh Market (Weekly)**
    - **When:** Every Tuesday year-round
    - **Where:** Moreton-in-Marsh, North Cotswolds
    - **Why Go:** Historic market town market dating back centuries, offering local crafts, fresh produce, antiques, and artisan foods. Perfect for a Tuesday visit.
    - **Cost:** Free entry; purchases vary.

Summer 2025

- **Tetbury Woolsack Races**
    - **When:** Saturday, July 19, 2025
    - **Where:** Tetbury
    - **Why Go:** A quirky and fun local tradition where contestants race carrying heavy sacks of wool up and down steep hills—a great spectacle of local spirit and physical challenge.
    - **Cost:** Free to watch; food and drinks available in local pubs.

- **Bourton-on-the-Water River Festival**
    - **When:** August 2–3, 2025
    - **Where:** Bourton-on-the-Water
    - **Why Go:** Celebrates the village's iconic river with boat races, stalls, live music, and family-friendly activities. The

village is one of the most picturesque spots in the Cotswolds.
- **Cost:** Free entry.

Autumn 2025

- **Cotswold Harvest Festival & Food Fairs**
    - **When:** September to October 2025 (various dates)
    - **Where:** Multiple locations including Cirencester, Stow-on-the-Wold
    - **Why Go:** Celebrate the bountiful harvest with farmers' markets, food tastings, and demonstrations highlighting local produce like apples, cheeses, and game meats.
    - **Cost:** Mostly free; food purchases vary.

- **Stroud Fringe Festival**
    - **When:** October 10–19, 2025
    - **Where:** Stroud
    - **Why Go:** An alternative arts festival featuring live music, theatre, art exhibitions, and workshops, perfect for those seeking cultural variety.
    - **Cost:** Events range from free to £15.

Winter 2025–2026

- **Cotswold Winter Walks & Christmas Markets**
    - **When:** November–December 2025
    - **Where:** Cirencester, Tetbury, Cheltenham
    - **Why Go:** Enjoy festive markets selling local crafts, artisan food, mulled wine, and seasonal gifts. The winter landscape adds to the cozy atmosphere of historic towns.
    - **Cost:** Free to enter markets; costs depend on purchases.

- **Cheltenham Christmas Market**
    - **When:** Late November to December 24, 2025
    - **Where:** Cheltenham Promenade
    - **Why Go:** Large, well-organized Christmas market with a range of stalls, entertainment, and local delicacies. Ideal for picking up unique gifts and experiencing festive cheer.
    - **Cost:** Free entry.

Public Transport Timetables: Key Routes in the Cotswolds

Traveling around the Cotswolds by public transport is practical but requires some planning due to rural routes and limited frequencies. Here's a breakdown of key bus and train routes to help you navigate efficiently.

Train Services

- **Oxford to Moreton-in-Marsh (via Kingham or Charlbury)**
    - **Operator:** Great Western Railway
    - **Frequency:** Hourly trains (approximate) from Oxford to Moreton-in-Marsh, with journey time around 45 minutes.
    - **Cost:** Advance single fares from £10, day returns approx. £15.
    - **Why Use:** Moreton-in-Marsh is a gateway to the northern Cotswolds and hosts the famous Tuesday market.

- **London Paddington to Cheltenham Spa**
    - **Operator:** Great Western Railway
    - **Frequency:** Several daily direct trains, journey time approx. 2 hours.
    - **Cost:** Advance fares from £25–£50 return.
    - **Why Use:** Cheltenham is a major hub for festivals, shopping, and historic sites.

- **Gloucester to Swindon (via Stroud, Kemble)**
    - **Operator:** Great Western Railway and local services
    - **Frequency:** Approximately hourly.
    - **Cost:** Single fares approx. £8–£15 depending on route.
    - **Why Use:** Useful for western Cotswolds access.

Bus Services

- **Stagecoach Bus X8: Cheltenham – Cirencester – Swindon**
    - **Frequency:** Hourly on weekdays; less frequent weekends.
    - **Cost:** Single fare approx. £6; day ticket £10.
    - **Why Use:** Connects key towns along the Cotswold edge, ideal for visitors exploring multiple destinations.

- **Pulhams Coaches 801: Moreton-in-Marsh – Stow-on-the-Wold – Bourton-on-the-Water**
    - **Frequency:** Several services daily, mainly focused on tourist season.
    - **Cost:** Single fare around £3–£5.
    - **Why Use:** Perfect for moving between classic villages on a day trip without a car.

- **Stagecoach Bus 855: Cirencester – Tetbury – Malmesbury**
    - **Frequency:** Less frequent, 4–6 services per day.
    - **Cost:** Single fares approx. £4–£7.
    - **Why Use:** Good for accessing southern Cotswold towns and villages.

Practical Tips for Using Public Transport in the Cotswolds

- **Advance Planning:** Bus services are less frequent on Sundays and bank holidays. Check timetables online via Stagecoach or Traveline websites ahead of your visit.
- **Ticket Options:** Consider day passes or group tickets if traveling with companions to save money.
- **Connections:** Some villages have limited service; consider combining trains with local taxis or bike rentals for last-mile travel.
- **Apps:** Use National Rail Enquiries and bus company apps for real-time updates.
- **Parking & Park & Ride:** For easier access, park in larger towns with good public transport links, such as Cheltenham or Moreton-in-Marsh, and take buses to smaller villages.

Summary

The Cotswolds' events calendar offers rich, seasonal experiences that bring the region's history, culture, and community spirit alive—whether it's a literary festival, quirky local races, or festive Christmas markets. Timing your visit around these can add a unique dimension to your trip.

Meanwhile, public transport is workable but best suited for travelers with flexible schedules and a bit of advance planning. The combination of train hubs and local bus routes makes day trips between towns and villages feasible without a car, but frequencies can be limited, especially on weekends.

Driving & Parking Guide for the Cotswolds

Why Drive in the Cotswolds?

Driving is arguably the best way to explore the Cotswolds if you want full flexibility and the ability to reach off-the-beaten-path villages, secluded manor houses, and countryside walks. Public transport, while reliable between major towns, can be sparse in rural areas, especially on weekends. With a car, you can create your own pace, visit multiple spots in a day, and discover hidden gems that buses don't reach.

What It's Like to Drive in the Cotswolds

- **Scenic but Narrow Roads:** Most routes are single-lane country roads with dry stone walls, hedgerows, and tight bends. Expect to slow down around blind corners, and be ready to reverse slightly to allow others to pass.
- **Driving Etiquette:** Locals are generally patient, but courteous driving is expected—wave when someone lets you pass and always slow down near horses, cyclists, or walkers.
- **Speed Limits:** Most village roads are 20–30 mph, while country roads are 60 mph, though in practice, you'll rarely reach that due to curves and visibility.
- **Fuel Costs:** Petrol prices in rural areas are typically higher than in urban centres. Expect around £1.55–£1.70 per litre, which is roughly £6.90–£7.70 per gallon (as of 2025). Fuel stations are in most towns: Cirencester, Stow-on-the-Wold, Bourton-on-the-Water, and Chipping Norton.

Car Hire

- **Major Rentals:** Available at Oxford, Cheltenham, Gloucester, and even London (for those combining city and countryside).
- **Recommended Hire Locations for Cotswold Visitors:**
    - **Oxford Railway Station** – ideal for starting a northern loop.
    - **Cheltenham Spa** – perfect for western Cotswolds.
- **Cost:** Expect around £45–£70 per day for a compact car with full insurance. Automatic cars are more expensive and should be booked in advance.

Parking in Major Cotswold Towns

Here's a breakdown of where to park and what it costs:

1. Bourton-on-the-Water

- **Car Parks:** Station Road Pay & Display (GL54 2AA)

- **Cost:** £2.30 for 2 hours, £5.50 for all-day parking
- **Tip:** Arrive before 10:30 am in peak season (May–Sept) to get a spot

2. Stow-on-the-Wold

- **Car Parks:** Market Square (free, but fills fast), Maugersbury Road (GL54 1BX)
- **Cost:** £1.40 for 2 hours, £3.40 all day
- **Tip:** Market days (usually Thursdays) make parking harder—arrive early or park on outskirts.

3. Cirencester

- **Car Parks:** Abbey Grounds (GL7 2BX), Forum Car Park
- **Cost:** £1.60 per hour, £6.50 full day
- **Tip:** Use Cirencester's RingGo app for hassle-free cashless parking.

4. Broadway

- **Car Parks:** Milestone Ground Car Park (WR12 7HA)
- **Cost:** £2.50 for 2 hours, £4.50 for 5+ hours
- **Tip:** Combine parking with lunch—some eateries offer partial reimbursement with a meal.

5. Tetbury

- **Car Parks:** Old Rail Yard (GL8 8DG)
- **Cost:** £1.00 per hour, £4.00 all day
- **Tip:** Great base for visiting Westonbirt Arboretum (10 mins drive)

Parking in Smaller Villages

In lesser-known spots like Swinbrook, Snowshill, or Painswick, parking can be more limited:

- Village Green or Church-side parking is common—usually free but please be considerate of residents.
- Always avoid blocking gates or narrow lanes, and look for designated lay-bys.

Tips for Hassle-Free Driving in the Cotswolds

- **Use a GPS or SatNav but don't rely solely on it**—mobile signal is weak in some rural areas. Download offline maps.
- **Pack coins or use parking apps like RingGo or PayByPhone**—many car parks still don't accept contactless or cards.
- **Avoid peak arrival hours (11 am–1 pm) during school holidays and weekends**—especially in July, August, and Easter.
- **Don't rush the journey.** Allow time between stops. What looks like a 20-minute drive may take 40+ minutes on winding lanes.

Road Closures & Events

- Check ahead during spring/summer for local festivals (like Burton's River Festival or Tetbury's Woolsack Races), which can cause temporary road closures and parking restrictions.
- Use Gloucestershire Highways or local council websites to check updates.

EV (Electric Vehicle) Drivers

- **Charging Points:** Found in Cirencester (Beeches Car Park), Cheltenham, Moreton-in-Marsh, and larger hotels.

- **Tip:** Use the Zap-Map app to find live EV availability.

Summary

Driving in the Cotswolds is not only practical but also one of the most scenic and rewarding ways to explore the area. With its honey-stone villages, panoramic hilltop views, and charming lanes, the region is tailor-made for a road trip. Just be mindful of narrow roads, plan for parking in advance, and embrace the slow travel pace that the Cotswolds encourages.

Made in the USA
Middletown, DE
12 July 2025